THIS BOOK IS FOR YOU...

because as a fully paid-up member of the human race, you are now entitled to access all the information in the world!

Increasingly this leaves many of us overwhelmed as we suffer from massive and often detrimental 'information overload', whether in our personal or work lives, or worse still, both.

Does this sound all too familiar?

- 'Your email inbox is nearly full' message frequently pops up on your computer, phone or tablet

- You just want the information of value for that all-important meeting or presentation, but cannot find it!

- You are sinking under the volume of 'stuff' coming at you 24/7!

This book is designed to give you the really big picture about information in the world in which we live today and the growing problem of information overload.

Most importantly, it will empower you with all the practical advice and guidance you need to control and get massive value from the information in your life - and not to let that information take over your life.

By reading this book, you will very quickly turn your information world around so that it will motivate you, move your life forward and remove the stress and curse of information overload.

Enjoy!

"Information overload is a symptom of our desire to not focus on what's important. It is a choice."

Brian Solis

What they are saying about Ron G Holland

"…..the incredible Ron G Holland, quite possibly the very greatest business and self development guru in Britain."

Fleet Street Publications

"I have been an associate of Ron Holland's for over twenty-five years and have seen Ron pull more rabbits out of hats for more clients, than anyone else I know."

Des Vadgama

"Be in no doubt that his work ethic, ability to cut through the jargon while stimulating that bio-supercomputer will leave you amazed."

Tim T Dingle BSc (Hons) PGCE MBA

"The constant dilemma of
the information age
is that our ability to
gather a sea of data
greatly exceeds the
tools and techniques
available to sort, extract,
and apply the information
we've collected."

Jeff Davidson

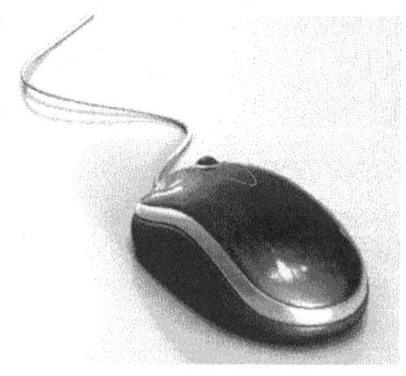

Dedication

This book is dedicated to Tim Berners-Lee who enhanced our lives by giving us the World Wide Web and fingertip access to all the information we need.

It is also dedicated to my wonderful daughter Kay, who embraces the 'information age' and everything it has to offer at every chance she gets.

Other titles by Ron G Holland

- The Eureka! Enigma
- Talk & Grow Rich
- Turbo Success
- Debt Free With Financial Kung Fu
- Escape From Where I Am
- Insider Secrets of Raising Capital for Business
- Retail & Grow Rich
- How to Earn Big Fat Fees from Niche Market Consultancy
- Cash Flow Magic - The Real Secret of Multiple Streams of Income
- Big In Britain
- Goal Setting that Really Works
- Isn't That Pyramid Selling?
- Kids with Two Brains – children's book series

About Ron G Holland

Ron G Holland is a seasoned entrepreneur, age 64, is a leading Motivational Speaker, Top Biz Guru and the Entrepreneur's Entrepreneur. Ron is one of the world's leading exponents on the subject of thinking and non-thinking. He gives numerous seminars and presentations and has been interviewed by TV, radio and the press on four continents.

He specialises in raising equity funding for early stage and start-up companies. His passion is fast cars, motorcycles and speedboats.

Ron has been at the cutting edge of personal development and self-help for over 30 years. He is the author of many business books, manuals and audio programs including *Talk & Grow Rich* and *Turbo Success* and *The Eureka! Enigma*. His first book, *Debt Free with Financial Kung Fu* was published in 1977 and his audio programs, including *Escape From Where I Am are*, in every prison library in the UK, and have been highly acclaimed.

Ron became a motivational speaker in 1981 when *Talk & Grow Rich* was first published in the USA.

Acknowledgements

This book was a grand team effort but in particular I would like to thank David Kellas and Jon Finegold for their diligent and prodigious output.

I would also like to thank my publisher Chris Day of Filament Publishing Ltd for his help and guidance throughout the project.

To connect with Ron G Holland,

visit the following:

www.RonHollandDirect.com

Information OVERLORD

How to Master the 'Information Age'

RON G HOLLAND

Published by
Filament Publishing Ltd
16, Croydon Road, Waddon,
Croydon, Surrey, CR0 4PA, United Kingdom
Telephone +44 (0)20 8688 2598
Fax +44 (0)20 7183 7186
info@filamentpublishing.com
www.filamentpublishing.com

© Ron G Holland 2013

The right of Ron G Holland to be identified as the author of this work has been asserted by him in accordance with the Designs and Copyright Act 1988.

ISBN 978-1-908691-93-4

Printed by CreateSpace

This book is subject to international copyright and may not be copied in any way without the prior written permission of the publishers.

CHAPTERS

Foreword — 13

Introduction to Information Overlord — 15

Chapter 1 — 17
Information Overload

Chapter 2 — 35
Valuing and the Value of Information

Chapter 3 — 59
Adding Value to Information

Chapter 4 — 81
Retrieving Information

Chapter 5 — 101
The Tower of Babel

Chapter 6 — 117
Dissemination of Information

Chapter 7 — 135
Information Technology

Chapter 8 — 159
Information Management

Chapter 9 — 181
Online Information and Reputation Management

Chapter 10 205
A Mind of Information

Chapter 11 223
Presenting Information Effectively

Chapter 12 255
Creating Sustainability Intelligently and Globally

Chapter 13 291
Facets of Information

Conclusion 305

The Information Overlord's Toolkit 307

> "Where is the wisdom we have lost in knowledge? Where is the knowledge we have lost in information."
>
> *T.S. Eliot*

FOREWORD

I hope you find this an interesting and, above all, a *useful* book in helping you deal more effectively with, and getting more value from, information. I have enjoyed writing it - immensely. The intriguing thing is, that when I started the project I did not realise exactly how it would end up - because of the subject matter being so disparate, and meaning so many different things to each and everyone one of us. I can tell you, however, that it has ended up far better and, I believe, more helpful to you than I could have ever possibly imagined. I originally had a specific audience in mind, but as the project gathered momentum, and as I interviewed more and more people in my professional network whilst carrying out huge amounts of Internet research, it really did take on a life of its own. What I discovered were a number of things of extreme importance, and here are three things that jump out, above all others, that I consider top of the Information Overlord's list:

1. The massive amount of miscommunication and non-communication between the everyday man or woman in the office and the IT industry

2. Most businesspeople do not understand the true value of the information and other intangible assets that they own and control

3. Sustainability and global warming are major issues for the 'Information industry'; by using this book as an oar, you will be able to steer in the right direction

By the time I reached the end of this book, and as a result of the insights I uncovered during my research journey, my target audience had changed considerably. I now believe the *Information Overlord* is a must-read for all those drawn to the title for whatever reason - more so for the man in the street, not just those with a technical bent or from an IT-related background. This book isn't about heaping more and more information on you, far from it. It is specifically designed to help you, in hundreds of different ways, to cope with and harness the 'information age' in which we live. From top-down and from bottom-up, yes, there is something for everyone involved in the IT industry - but more from a practical customer need perspective. I also hope that my book will act as the catalyst to create stronger empathy between the Information Technology expert and the people they have to help (like me!) every day of the week.

Ron G Holland
London 2013

> "We have for the first time an economy based on a key resource [Information] that is not only renewable, but self-generating. Running out of it is not a problem, but drowning in it is." *John Naisbitt*

An introduction to the 'Information Age'

INTRODUCTION TO INFORMATION OVERLORD

I like the story of the billionaire who frequently advertised that he'd pay a million dollars to anyone who can tell him where he will die. When he was quizzed on why he would do such a thing, he simply replied, "Once I know where I'm going to die, I shall never go there." Some information is worth a lot of money.

Some Useless Information!

1. A rat can last longer without water than a camel.
2. The dot over the letter 'I' is called a tittle.
3. Roses may be red, but violets are always violet.
4. There is not a single word in the dictionary that rhymes with orange, purple or silver.
5. If one places a tiny amount of liquor on a scorpion, it will instantly go mad and sting itself to death.
6. The name Wendy was made up for the book *Peter Pan*.
7. A female ferret will die if it goes into heat and cannot find a mate.
8. Charlie Chaplin once won third prize in a Charlie Chaplin lookalike contest.

9. Celery has negative calories. It takes more calories to digest a piece of celery than the celery has in it to begin with.

10. The original name for butterfly was flutterby.

Some information has no value.

I will deliberately keep this book short and sweet; half of the problem, these days, is that too many people waffle on, trying to justify their own existence - when, really, they could reduce what they are saying to the salient points, and then leave the reader to decide whether they want to drill down deeper into any particular topic. The trouble, today, is that it's just too easy to waffle, to too many people!

The purpose of this book is to articulate a number of issues that exist all around us in this information era, so that we may live happier, more productive, and meaningful lives - without getting bogged down in things that really don't matter.

> "It's not information overload.
> It's filter failure."
> *Clay Shirky*

CHAPTER 1

INFORMATION OVERLOAD

"It is paradoxical, but the mind is more creative when it is less active"

Ron G Holland

The title of this book is INFORMATION OVERLORD, but my research has already shown me that many people will impulsively buy a copy because they erroneously believe its title to be INFORMATION OVERLOAD.

Information Overload is something that is almost impossible to avoid, whether it be at home or in the office. One thing, for sure, is that you will never become an Information Overlord if you suffer from it. So we will attempt to address this debilitating issue first and foremost.

Dictionary Definition: Information overload

> 'Stress induced by reception of more information than is necessary to make a decision (or that can be readily understood and digested in the time available) and by attempts to deal with it with outdated time management practices.'
>
> *(www.businessdictionary.com)*

Clearly this is a condition that you want to avoid, so that you can just get on with your life in a productive way, whether it is at a personal or business environment level.

Where does it all come from?

From the time you wake up, to the moment your head hits the pillow, you will be bombarded by, literally, billions of pieces of information - or *data* as your built-in biocomputer (your brain) will see it - that need to be translated into meaningful, preferably actionable output. But how can you make sure this 'translation' happens? And how can you make sure that the valuable stuff never gets lost? Later in this book, I will go into much more detail about how to address these issues that I believe are now at endemic levels, particularly within businesses - both large and small - where, potentially, many millions of pounds are being lost through poor information management and often wanton neglect.

I am sure that you will be able to come up with a list of the sources of information that give you the most pain in your life, whether at home or in the office. Here are just a few worth logging, some clearly with an inherently low value attached - and others with potentially millions hidden away in their description!

- Background TV noise
- Chatter in public places
- Spam email
- Personal email
- Business reports, case studies
- Personal headphones - other people's
- Newspapers
- Internal/external work email
- Historical research reports
- Social media trails - Facebook, Twitter

The negative impact of information overload

The problem with information today is that there is too much of it, making it extremely difficult to sort out the wheat from the chaff. The valuable stuff can very easily get lost, unless you rigorously manage your information flow daily. Leave it too long and this will become an impossible task, as I am sure you know!

The good news is that there are some basic things that you can do **NOW** to begin the journey towards becoming an **INFORMATION OVERLORD:**

1. **Assimilating Information**

Learn how to do professional research and also how to speed read. When I get the bit between my teeth on a project, I usually use a number of different search engines and then end up saving all the relevant pages. I then speed read these, at my leisure, in complete silence with no distractions, looking for gems and clues that may help me in my quest of getting to the bottom of the subject of the topic in hand. Many schools in the UK now teach pupils how to assimilate information and conduct research - skills that are, sadly, lacking in so many of us.

2. **No-Mind**

I have been writing about 'no-mind' for over 30 years and it really is the key to information overload - as well as creativity, generating solutions, ideas and Eurekas! The Japanese have a name for no-mind - 'Satori'. They have been practicing the art for thousands of years. To find out more about "stopping the internal dialogue and hearing the Eurekas!" check out *Turbo Success* and my later book, *The Eureka! Enigma*. In essence, in silence, stillness and solitude, you can hear your 'small still voice' which is the voice of your subconscious mind.

3. **We know too much**

It is highly likely you have more than enough information and knowledge in your own mind to accomplish the goals you have set yourself. I love Gnarls Barkley's song *Crazy*; the lyrics are spot on:

'it's not that I didn't know enough - I just knew too much!'

Listen to it...

4. Unsubscribe

Immediately unsubscribe from all free newsletters - and probably all others too - unless they are absolutely essential to your life or work.

5. Cancel all the newspapers

Most newspapers are full of negative, rehashed, overblown garbage that you could well do without. These days I just buy all of the newspapers on a Sunday - and allow just one hour to speed read them, mentally scan and see what is pertinent to me. I refuse to let the whole weekend get eaten up by other people's agendas.

6. Switch off the TV - or dump it altogether

I used to watch wall-to-wall news, 24/7. Other people are addicted to wall-to-wall soaps and others, wall-to-wall comedies. Whatever you're addicted to, have yourself a wake-up call. Stop stuffing yourself with all this unnecessary input.

7. Other people's agendas

The majority of emails, offers and texts that you are getting are other people's agendas being foisted upon you; they are distracting you from your own agenda. Delete all emails without reading - unless *absolutely* essential.

8. Multi-tasking

This is a word that describes the action of being able to carry out many tasks at the same time. The problem is that I have never seen anyone do a serious job of work being able to multitask! Really productive people usually work all through the night, when the phones are silent, the emails are shut off and every other imaginable distraction is locked away and buttoned down. They can then start the serious business of work; writing a book, creating a song, developing some advertising copy or writing a robust business plan.

9. Eliminate gold baubles

Take time to eliminate all pop-ups, adverts and any other distractions, no matter what guise or form they come in. These days you can see hundreds of images an hour on your computer, mobile phone or other device. All these are what I call the 'gold bauble syndrome' - they will keep dragging you away from your work task or labour of love.

10. Text messages or social media contacts

Because they tend to be free, people use this far too often and, in most instances, for trivia. Each time a text message or social media contact arrives, it has the capability of overloading you with useless information and detracts you from an important job in hand. Each and every one of us only has so much mental bandwidth - why let it get used up with things that don't count?

11. Other people's phone calls

If you are unfortunate enough to share buses, trains and coaches with people who insist on making and accepting phone calls (and invariably speaking at the top of their voices), you need to find a way to counter this invasion of privacy and preventing this garbage entering your neurons. Move away from the person, put on headphones and play classical music, or possibly a stimulating self-help or personal development track.

12. Respond to your emails at the beginning and end of each day

In the good old days, the snail mail used to get delivered at 9am; we would respond to our letters and then wait until the next day for another delivery. These days we are faced with a constant barrage of incoming email, texts and voicemail; if you tend to reply to them as they arrive, your working day will get severely disrupted and eaten in to. The only effective way is to become highly disciplined and attend to email at the beginning and end of each day, leaving your hands and brain free for productive and creative work. Learn this secret sooner rather than later, so you can increase your productivity and reduce your information overload.

13. Other people's noise (OPN)

For years I have been writing about, not only OPM (Other People's Money) but OPN which is Other People's Noise. I advocate buying malleable wax earplugs by the box-load, as well as adding earmuffs and white noise. It is crucial to get quiet downtime and block out other people's noise so you can listen to the 'small still voice' which is the all-important voice of your subconscious mind!

14. Get yourself a Mentor

Getting yourself a business mentor is a crucial part of overcoming overload because, if they are any good, they will immediately help you to start focusing on just one or two things that really count.

15. What would you do if you were performing well?

A worthwhile exercise is writing down, on as many A4 sheets as it takes, a profile of what your life would look like and what you would accomplish if you were performing well. I am sure that it is going to include 'getting away from it all' so that you can start doing creative and productive work. Just try it - it'll be a big wake-up call.

ZOOM SECRETS

Every chapter throughout my book includes a discreet set of key highlights that I like to call *'Zoom Secrets'*. They provide specific action points that you can easily apply in your home or business life. Most importantly, they also provide the roadmap to becoming a true 'Information Overlord'.

We are all different; we work in different ways, in different situations, and with different people. Only **YOU** know what could be possible for you - but don't fall into the trap of thinking "I won't try that - it'll never work for me!" Try it!

It costs nothing to try a new way of doing things - if you try something and it doesn't work, then go back to your original way of working, and try to think of an alternative!

Your Personal Action Plan (1)

The antidote to Information Overload is learning to live your life in an entirely different way; even if you feel you are currently suffering, you'll be glad you did. Here are just a few things to begin with. Start practising these and an alternative mode of living will evolve...

1. Become a whole-brain thinker

Many of the older generation tend to be left-brain thinkers - that is how they were educated and brought up. This older generation needs to start thinking in pictures as much as they do in words and begin to access both sides of the brain.

The modern generation are brought up on a stiff diet of computer games, consoles, television and picture books and are now becoming predominantly right-brained. This generation needs to harness the left brain and think in words, as much as they do in pictures.

Are you a left or right-brain thinker? Start by noting down what you normally do when under pressure - do you start by planning in a logical manner (left-brain thinker) or try and think creatively about a solution to the problem (right-brain thinker)?

2. Become conscious

Most folk, these days, are totally 'unconscious', being caught up in their own fast-moving world, for most part not realising what is going on around them.

The Information Overlord will take pains to create an environment that is conducive to creativity and happiness. Note down here how you will set about doing this:

3. Embrace the countryside

By taking full days out, not just 10 or 15 minutes, away from towns and cities. Leave all mobile devices behind; this frightens most people, as they just can't stand being without communication and music for more than a few seconds. Learn how to listen to the noises of the world and appreciate bird song, wildlife, wind, snow, rain as well as sun. Take joy from the forests, hills and river walks where you can hear the 'small still voice' from within.

Note down three places that you will visit over the next two months:

1.

2.

3.

4. Eat slower, eat right

For many years I had been caught up in the fast-paced information era and had become accustomed to ordering fast food because there wasn't enough time in the day. It wasn't until I started taking regular trips to Bulgaria that I developed a taste for their incredible Shopska salad. Not only do I take my time making the salads, but I also enjoy eating them - very slowly - with the full knowledge that eating salads is all part of being an Information Overlord.

If you haven't yet discovered a salad that turns you on, perhaps it's time to experiment with a few vegetables and dressings that you really enjoy and leave out all the ingredients that you don't.

5. Drive slower, walk faster

The information age has got us all into an unnecessary tizzy and the Information Overlord needs to extract him or herself from this hectic pace of life and be in this world, but not of it. Slow down and enjoy things more, enjoy the journey as well as the destination

Identify three things that you will do differently in your day-to-day home and business life that will help you slow down and lead a safer and healthier existence:

1.

2.

3.

6. Start single tasking

I embrace the solitude I have created for myself and focus my attention on just this one project. I know that single tasking is the way to harness creativity in everything that I do.

What five things can you do to create your own 'information overload free' personal time to enable you to focus on one important task in your life?

1.

2.

3.

4.

5.

7. Start removing distractions from your life

What could you do - now - that would remove some distractions?

List here five things you could - and will! - try:

1.

2.

3.

4.

5.

8. Create a list of important tasks for each day/week/month and focus only on the most important one until completed

Start now - and get into the habit of making a brief list, each evening, of 'Things I must do...'

List the key things you need to do..

Tomorrow:

This week.....

.....and all the things that you must do this month...

9. Every day, introduce one change that will free you from overload

Take a moment to think about this requirement. What could you do? List five ideas, but come back to this section to jot ideas when they occur to you.

1.

2.

3.

4.

5.

CHAPTER 2

VALUING AND THE VALUE OF INFORMATION

"The value is that which the decision maker is willing to pay"

Ron G Holland

The Information Overlord knows the value of working out exactly how much, to the penny, his information is worth - not just to himself, but also to others. It is important to think as widely as possible when carrying out this critical exercise. Your information may be worth, say, £1,000 to you - but in a competitor's hands, it might be worth 10 or 100 times that amount. This would clearly put things in a completely different light when it comes to reviewing data and information security processes that you may currently have in place - at home or in the workplace.

It is crucial to examine the value of information in business, as it is frequently overlooked and undervalued; the individuals managing it are rarely in a position to understand its true worth.

Take, for example, the database of new leads that has been painfully created over a six-month period, via salesmen in the field, targeted marketing activity, as well as names and addresses purchased from mailing list companies. The database manager might have ultimate control over this, but will have not calculated the overall staff time in its cost of development, the marketing costs or the value of any new business that might come in from the leads. The sum of all these parts equals the true value of the information. And, if those leads were then to accidentally or deliberately get into the hands of a major competitor, what is then the **lost** value to the business?

Demystify the value

We must demystify the 'valuation of information' and bring about some clarity of thought that articulates just how this much-overlooked asset should be valued. Simple processes can be put in place to carry out a top-line value analysis exercise.

This would involve (a) identifying and documenting the key stakeholders in the value chain, and then (b) seeing how they use a particular type of information to help them make decisions. Those decisions will normally have a commercial value attached, and can be used to positively offset the initial cost of acquiring the information.

Here are a few good places to start the ball rolling:

Checking out people and companies: These days you don't need too much information to be able to carry out a thorough due diligence on people and companies that you intend to deal with. Making the right decisions in the early stages of relationships can be crucial - whether it be hiring a new top executive or partnering with a new business-critical supplier.

If you are in possession of a simple business card, it quickly gets you onto the digital trail that people leave behind them. You can check to see if the address tallies with published sources; you can see if there are any loans on the property and you can look at Companies House for the details on the company - as well any other companies that person is associated with. You can really get to the bottom of potential partners, whether they are suppliers, outsourcers, customers, investors, professional advisers or employees. One hour's worth of diligent research tucked under your belt and you can go into a deal or relationship with your eyes wide open - and know which questions to ask, and where to probe further.

Valuable information is out there and readily available; it may save you from serious fraud, heartache or many hours of executive time and, therefore, cost to your business. If it isn't there, that will tell you something as well!

In the boardroom: Information is crucial in any decision-making process and it should not be on the Chief Information Officer's (CIO) shoulders alone to understand the types of information available and how to use it. The Chairman, Chief Executive and Finance Director, as well as their staff, should all have a level of understanding as to how much has been invested in the information in the first place - and how it can be used to create value in the future.

The CIO is no longer master of information technology. He or she must become a master (mistress?) of information management - indeed they must become Information Overlords! To be of real value, the data collected and provided to support business decisions (such as planning, consolidations, disposals, fundraising, acquisitions, budgeting, market intelligence, competitor intelligence and business and customer feedback) needs, in most instances, to be simplified much more than it currently is.

Today the pace is often so fast you do not get time for a leisurely read of background papers, but many times can only scan tabled information an hour or two before a meeting. In busy organisations, *less* information is often valued higher, because it is actually read and assimilated more easily. The Information Overlord will excel in the art of creating bite-sized information chunks that meet the needs of key decision makers.

The more accurate, simple and, if appropriate, visually creative the information that board directors and managers have, the better they are able to reduce any uncertainty that comes with every business decision. If you can eliminate uncertainty in your inventory, your working capital can be optimised. Inventory management can be turned into lean best practice, all driven by demand. It is the *value* of information that transforms an IT department from a shared-cost centre to a profit centre in its own right, by measuring the contribution from IT to business success and bottom-line profit.

Marketing: I discovered, a long time ago, that market information needs to be very short and concise, even when marketing to prospects, clients, brokers and venture capitalists. These days we are more concerned with what designers, editors and copywriters can produce rather than long sophisticated reports and business plans with reams of market data from accountants and lawyers. Our *raison d'être* is to leave prospects and customers with their tongues hanging out, begging for more: "Please can we have a business plan? Please can we have more information?"

Only then do we know we've got them! Long gone are the days of overwhelming people with boring business plans, full of market statistics, the size of telephone directories. We are in the 'information age' but it is more frequently becoming a case of 'less is more'.

Accountancy methods of the industrial age

In the industrial age, accountancy methodology was to account for goods first, money second and lastly, if at all, information. This was way down the list of priorities, reflecting the industrial economy at the time.

Accountants were tasked to make sure all was in alignment. In the industrial era, *tangible assets* were the major source of value - but their values deteriorated with use. In the 'information age', by contrast, most value comes from information that can frequently increase in value with usage. In the twenty-first century, in many organisations, both small and large, it is *information flow* that has become the primary focus; the supply of goods can often be further down in the pecking order. Frequently money flow is just an exchange of information, amounting to blips on a screen. It is information that drives value, not product. The axiom of *location, location, location* has now been changed to *database, database, database.*

There are, today, many ways to turn information into profit centres; IT departments are - or should be - increasingly called upon to help businesses make money by helping to extract real value from data and information - not just offering technical support services.

How do you value anything?

I remember asking my first business mentor, the loquacious Seamus O'Rourke, about the secret of valuing companies; with a wry grin, he replied, "Be Jeezus, Ronnie, it all depends whether you're buying or selling!"

Company valuations depend on many things; frequently market considerations can wipe out or add huge amounts to valuations. In the 1980s I remember a print company was about to float, when it was rumoured they were laundering money for a terrorist organisation. The price collapsed. A pharmaceutical company was recently rumoured to be taking over another; the share price rose dramatically.

At a recent Sotheby's auction in Hong Kong, a cobalt blue Ming vase sold for a record $21.6 million. How come this piece of pottery gained many millions in value in under five minutes? Supply and demand is the simple answer. Like any commodity, it is worth *what people are willing to pay for it*. When you have a room full of bidders and additional bids coming in over the telephone and Internet, you have set the scene for a buying frenzy. To get price hikes like this, you need at least two bidders - and preferably quite a few more.

To value a commodity

In the field of economics, the commodity value of a good is its 'free market intrinsic value under optimal use conditions'.

In a free market, the commodity value of a good is reflected by its price. For example, if an acre of land can yield $50 gain by being planted with corn, and $100 gain by being planted with strawberries or tomatoes, then that acre's *commodity value* is $100. At the end of the day maybe the landowner will go for Saffron or grape vines, pushing the commodity value even higher.

An elegant formula

When it comes to valuing intangibles (which includes information), there are a number of variables to take into consideration. Kjetil Tonstad states that, "the value of information is the difference between the project value with the information and the project value without the information, minus the cost of acquiring the information."

This is clearly an elegant solution to the question of valuation and one that will work for discreet projects - but may not be so good for more transient commercial activities that rely heavily on data and information.

Raw or refined?

Mining companies value their discovered but undeveloped reserves. Gold that is mined from the ground has one value; it has another value once it is refined, and yet an increased value when it is fashioned into jewellery. Gold that has been crafted into *Cartier* jewellery has a yet higher value.

Information can be viewed the same way and has many states. Very much like ore that is still deep in the ground, much will depend on what it costs to discover, extract, refine and process into information with real decision-making value.

What will it cost to replace?

You may care (and I would certainly recommend you do) to analyse the cost of what it has taken to accumulate all the information that you own. You may be surprised at the true dollar cost when you take into account the work that goes into data collection: PR, advertising, surveys, research, phone calls to clients and customers, analysis, data entry, merging and purging and continually updating. Be careful to avoid duplication of effort as this is a common occurrence in data collection.

The end result of this exercise will be to give you the perfect starting point to quantify the true value of your 'information estate'.

What will someone pay for it?

Is there someone who will pay you for the information that you have? You can research and see what others are getting for similar types of information. Will you rent your information for a one-time use - or will you sell it as a business or as a complete going concern?

You may decide to share your information free of charge of course, should your objective be to raise your profile or credibility within your market niche to indirectly gain product or brand revenue. This is common practice these days and the mainstay of many an Internet marketing campaign.

Customers and consumers love anything that is *free;* the trick is to provide a hook using the free information to draw them into making a purchase from your range of wonderful products!

Time allotted to value the information

Set specific time limits of either internal or external audits on valuation of intangible assets and information. Otherwise a valuation of information can take forever and end up costing more in time and effort than the information is actually worth!

I am minded of some great conversation I had with my business partner of 25 years, Bruce Snyder, who was a scientist, physicist and mathematician. He worked on projects such as Skylab, Stingray torpedo, Exocet missile systems and even the communication system for Whitehall. He noted that, whenever a report was due, it would take months and months - and inevitably only get finished on the eve of the deadline. Bruce came to the conclusion that all the project time was spent gathering intelligence and only, at the eleventh hour, would everyone sit down and come up with a consensus opinion. The process of valuing information can frequently follow these exact same lines unless you, as the Information Overlord, put in place a few key milestones to monitor and review progress. Remember, the outcome should provide an insight into the value of the information you have - not reams and reams of more analysis.

How much money will it make you over a period of time?

The information that you own as intellectual property could either make you rich - or just cost you money to store and maintain. Clearly you want to receive the value and not just the cost! Here are a few more tips on how you can generate an excellent income, month after month, from the IP rights you have worked hard to achieve, and that can then form the basis of your information valuation exercise:

- Renting out to other users on a one-time or long-term basis. At its simplest, this is the principle behind the sale of email or contact lists

- Offering your data and knowledge on a 'continuous' basis to small or large companies that do not have the resources to produce it themselves - many large multi-million pound turnover data and insight organisations have started in just this way. Again, this was the basis behind the concept of franchises - someone worked out to do something (print, make burgers, create wedding dresses) and then sold the concept in to other people

- Writing an eBook and having it sold on Amazon or Clickbank - or creating an app for a smartphone

- Extending your first successful eBook to series two, three or even four!

How much will it cost to maintain it at optimum level?

Some information will need cleaning, merging and purging, updating, using, insuring, duplicating and securing. All this means a cost in time and money and adds to the cost of the information in the first place. On occasion, the price of maintaining information way exceeds the value of it - you do not want to fall into this trap!

Patents are a good way of protecting information and securing your intellectual property - but they also cost money to file and uphold. This can run into many thousands of pounds, especially if you are trying to secure worldwide patents.

This may well be worth investing in, though, if your information is unique and has a likely high return. To establish if this is the case, carry out some customer or consumer research before you start spending more money, in order to establish likely demand.

Has it passed the point of no return?

The 'point of no return' is, when you are on a journey, you have gone past the halfway stage; it no longer makes sense to return to base, because it is actually shorter to head to your destination. Has your information reached the point of no return, has it passed its sell-by-date? You need to be honest with yourself here. Again, as I said earlier, carrying out some research with your likely client or customer base will establish if what you have is actually 'of the moment' or way out of date. Or worse, a competitor has got there before you, and as a result, has made your information offering or service obsolete.

Valuable if accurate?

When NASA used to do its moon shots, the data they used had to be 100% accurate otherwise the consequences would be disastrous. However, if a company decides to use a database to launch a new product via a mailshot, the information can be less accurate; most direct mail users expect response rates in the region of only one or two per cent. A lot of 'rejects' can be attributed to faulty addressing of the mail. If they had more accurate data, the response rate is likely to be higher and they would make more money from the campaign.

However, it does cost serious money to create highly accurate data. Once a company has sold product to a new database of customers and managed to achieve, maybe, a breakeven return on the deal of one per cent, it can look forward to selling *those* new customers the next round of products - and might expect a take-up of 15% or even 20%. And, in turn, the database of those customers (i.e. those purchasing for the second time) should eventually become highly prized by both yourself and any joint venture partners that you may have, due to its accuracy and quality. Over time, it can be developed into a repository of loyal consumers of your products and services; as an added bonus, these people are much more likely to recommend you to others than many of your 'one-off' customers might be.

List brokers value information at £100 per 1,000

List brokers usually rent specific lists of information, usually to non-competing vendors, on a one-time use only, for an average of around £100 per 1,000 names and addresses. These names are usually sent to you on a database that can be printed in any label format you desire.

The list owner, depending on demand, may put the price up by 15% or more but may, or may not, get takers if the perceived value to the customer has already peaked. Bear in mind as well that, if you were a buyer of this service, you may find yourself fishing in a pond of diminishing returns: the recipient of the mailshot only has so much money to spend and one day may not be able to buy anything at all if they have received too many advantageous offers already!

Is it compliant?

Unfortunately, I was recently involved in the abortive sale of a database company. The company in question had tracked and monitored for the period of over 25 years the top richest 40,000 people in the UK. It held records on databases and also owned its own hard copy press cuttings library - a huge amount of information. In *The Sunday Times* rich list you may get a single page about each individual but here, more often than not, there was 20, 30 or 40 pages of intelligence forming *each* profile. We attracted many offers, all in the millions - but, when it came down to due diligence, not a single buyer would put down cash because of the way the information had been gathered.

An honest and ethical approach to information collection and management is crucial in today's modern world; by following government data protection guidelines to the letter, individuals and companies in the information and data business will be able to gain maximum value from that information when the times comes to use it commercially.

How many 'eyeballs' on the information?

I can't recall the number of times when I was pulled aside and told, "No, no, it's not the number of subscribers that we talk about, it's the number of eyeballs viewing that information". So suddenly 30,000 subscribers became 60,000 eyeballs, I suppose just to add to the giddy mix of hyperbole that already existed. This 'eyeballs' thing went on for quite a few years and is still worth thinking about in terms of a quantifiable measure when it comes to evaluating how many people you have shared your information with.

Valuing 'eyeballs' in the early days of the Internet

I remember back to 1997, reading the story of how Bill Gates phoned Sabeer Bhatia, one of the co-founders of Hotmail, and offered him $200,000,000 for the company which had not a single dollar turnover. Sabeer turned him down! The story was that Sabeer's dad sternly told him that if Bill Gates ever phoned again, he was to take the offer.

Luckily, he did call again; the offer, this time, was an unprecedented $390million in Microsoft stock. Hotmail back then had an estimated 8.9 million subscribers; based on the Microsoft purchase price, each user was valued at over $40. Not bad, considering that none of those subscribers was paying anything for the service, nor did they have to register many personal details to get a Hotmail account.

To have made a valuation at that level in those giddy days, Billy boy must have done all sorts of sums; potential for the future, how many 'eyeballs', how big could it grow to under Microsoft's wing, what was the potential of the Internet - and also what could those free subscribers end up buying from Microsoft, and what could it do for Microsoft's market share and share value. When you consider that, until quite recently, Hotmail was the biggest email provider in the world (with some 364,000,000 subscribers, many of whom are paying for additional Microsoft products and services), Bill Gates clearly got something right. (Hotmail now combines Live.com and also Outlook.com)

The important thing to remember from all these facts is that the information, the database, was valued *at over $40 per subscriber.* This set a precedent for 'information-based' Internet deals and businesses to come. How much have you, as the Information Overlord, valued each of the recipients of your information services at? Future value is often more important than current value of course, so map out your plans and run a top-line forecast of likely revenues over a five-year period. You might be surprised as to how much each of your subscribers (and potential new subscribers) individual values will have grown.

Valuation of Facebook's information database - eyeballs don't even get a look in

Whilst in the process of writing this book, the world of finance is talking about the Internet flotation of the century. Facebook (as of September 2012) has a growing 900,000,000 non-fee paying subscribers and is not yet making a profit. Estimated market values following the Initial Public Offering (IPO) (when it eventually happens), are appearing all over the press and the Internet and range from $60billion up to an eye-watering $100billion. Some analysts are also saying that even at this level, Facebook appears undervalued! I tend to have some sympathy with this as a $100billion price equates to each subscriber having a net worth value of 'only' $125 in today's money. With the global reach that Facebook has, I would suggest that this should be nearer $200 per subscriber.

Potential contenders vying for the business include Microsoft, Google and Citi representing China and maybe tens of thousands of private investors all wanting a slice of the cherry pie and therefore helping to drive the share price continually upwards.

UNPRECEDENTED PUSH AND PULL POTENTIAL

Now netrepreneurs set values of their companies

Make no mistake about it, it does take some getting your mind around. How, in a few short years, a business can create 900,000,000 potential cash customers, from that number of free subscribers; that can all be contacted within seconds with the latest must-have offer. This would have massive value and netrepreneurs understand that - and they are the ones who can also see the future potential and how big Facebook and the whole social media trend can really be from a revenue-generating perspective.

Potential for the future sets values

You can quite easily deduce that, although a company may currently have no *turnover*, it will have massive *value* in terms of the consumer information it holds and has directly at its marketing fingertips. 900,000,000 subscribers, all who have entered inordinate amounts of information about themselves, either intentionally or unwittingly, about their birthdates, friends, family, likes and dislikes, hobbies, careers, health, clothes, make-up, buying habits, marital status, etc provides an unparalleled consumer relationship marketing (CRM) and future profit potential opportunity.

Precedents set values

Once a major information provider has either been sold or floated for a sum of money, it sets a precedent for similar sales or IPOs in the future. Suddenly, that type or category of information has a real or perceived value - and can be used to help set a benchmark for valuations of companies playing in that same space. Think about the type of information you or your business is managing - has a precedent to help you value *your* assets already been established?

You can easily see if a company gets a valuation of $100,000,000 (or even half a billion) because it may have attracted venture capital and has a certain number of subscribers, even if they are non-paying and the company has no turnover, let alone makes no profit. A search on Google will throw up most of the key facts you need to carry out your own benchmarking analysis.

What information is likely to have the highest value?

The saying 'straight from the horse's mouth' is worth quoting here. In a nutshell it means 'from the highest authority'. In horse racing circles, tips on which horse is likely to be a winner circulate amongst punters prior to a race. The most credible tips are considered to be from those in closest touch with the recent form of the horse, often the stable lads and trainers. The idiom 'from the horse's mouth' is supposed to indicate one step better than even that inner circle - the horse itself! Information gained from a primary source should always therefore be considered to be of the highest value.

In the world of consumer and market research, information and data is normally classified as being 'Primary' or 'Secondary'. Your own information can easily be classified in the same way so as to determine which has the most potential to reap the highest reward:

1. Primary information

When you ask a friend or colleague for their view on something, consider this to be a *primary information* source. On its own, of course, the information they give you is 'nice to know' - but not of any significant value as it is just one person's comment or view. However, if you ask the same question to, say, 150 people, suddenly it becomes more meaningful, qualitative in nature and therefore a valuable source of insight to help base decisions upon. Roll the same question out to a thousand more people and suddenly you are in a position to quantify your initial results and provide robust decision-making insights.

2. Secondary Information

Most of us these days search the Internet for information on any subject you may care to mention. For those who do not have access to the 'Net', good old-fashioned books and directories will most likely be the source they turn to. This type of information is typically classed as *secondary* and is used extensively by professional research companies to support projects that they may have been commissioned to undertake, sometimes prior to carrying out primary research. The value apportioned to secondary information, albeit it may take many weeks or sometimes months to compile, will normally be less than that attained via direct, quantified interaction with your potential customers or consumers.

ZOOM SECRETS

Your Personal Action Plan (2)

1. Know the value of your information

> It is crucial to examine the value of information in business, as it is frequently overlooked and undervalued; the individuals managing it are rarely in a position to understand its true worth.
>
> 1. Make a list of your most important information assets in the chart below. What are the top five (internal) sources of your information, such as (for example only) customer database, lists of products bought or sold (depending on your organisation); website statistics; etc
>
> 2. ...and then estimate the value of each information asset, taking into consideration time taken to create it, sales generated from that asset, the price of replacing the information in it, losses if it is lost, and what others would be willing to pay to you for that information.
>
> | Information Asset | Value (currency) |
> |---|---|
> | | |
> | | |
> | | |
> | | |
> | | |

2. Maintain, safely store and backup your valuable information assets

Your information may be worth, say, £1,000 to you - but in a competitor's hands, it might be worth 10 or 100 times that amount.

Some information will need cleaning, merging and purging, updating, using, insuring, duplicating and securing.

Create a simple strategy - maybe a set of five instructions - for securing, maintaining, managing and backing up your information.

1.

2.

3.

4.

5.

3. Identify ways to create value from your information

> *Brainstorm, with colleagues, better ways of monetising the information you have. Design a simple model of storing and presenting this information.*
>
> *Who can you sell or hire your database to?*

CHAPTER 3

ADDING VALUE TO INFORMATION

"To add value to information is twenty-first century alchemy"

Ron G Holland

There are multiple ways to add value to information and I suspect the majority of them have yet to be invented. Here are a few that may stimulate some ideas, and maybe some profit...

Research

This is one of marketing's most powerful, yet underutilised tools. Research is a hidden secret, if there ever was one - you, as an Information Overlord, will need to have this process totally sewn up.

There are numerous ways of conducting research. From an individual perspective, it will most often these days be about using the right website to find the product or service you are looking for. Holiday research in particular can be a full-time hobby for many people, using sites such as *www.tripadvisor.com* which provide valuable feedback from traveller's real-life experiences with different tour operators, hotels or holiday letting agencies.

When it comes to business, it can be as simple as questions being asked of consumers in the street, through to major blue-chip companies launching new products using consumer focus groups (a small number of people in a room with a moderator), online research and good old-fashioned questionnaires being mailed through the post.

To carry out robust business research, you need to have the right equipment for the job. Numerous websites, offering dedicated research tools, are springing up all over the Net, such as 'surveymonkey' and 'webpirate'; each fulfilling a valuable and effective service. Take advantage of them as, generally, they require minimal investment.

There is no doubt that gleaning accurate information about your desired holiday destination or, from a business perspective, the identified target consumer for a new product launch, can add huge value to the final outcome. It will ensure that the time, energy and money you have invested will have all been worthwhile.

Just-in-time, speed of delivery

Getting information to the right spot quickly adds huge value to information; this is handsomely demonstrated in places such as China and Japan, where the 'information culture' is completely different to that in the West. On many production lines, problems are flagged up to the workforce within minutes of a problem occurring. Unlike their western counterparts, everyone in the workforce has the right to bring a production line to a grinding halt; within 10 or 15 minutes of information being received, the line can be stopped, things remedied or repaired - and then started up again, making for tremendous overall efficiency. There is minimal wastage, maximum quality, minimum wasted staff time.

Clean it

It is very easy to build up volumes of information that quickly become out of date. You need a rigorous filing process, whether in electronic format for email, documents, etc. or paper-based for letters, journals, etc. On a regular basis, delete, destroy or archive information that is no longer adding value.

Databases can be enhanced by merging and purging and cleaning out all duplicated and dead addresses. If you don't regularly clean and update data, it quickly deteriorates, until one day it is rendered valueless.

Whichever way you look at it, cleaning and maintaining information to create long-term value does cost time and money, but is an essential part of becoming an Information Overlord.

Filter it

Don't let good data get contaminated with data from unverified sources. It's now easier than ever to put simple processes in place that automatically filter your personal and business mail, for example. Use the free Spam tools that your email service provider offers - or get your IT support people to set your mail system profile up so that you only get the mail you really need.

When it comes to larger, more valuable business reports and documents, make sure that the information used to support business cases or proposals are from trusted sources - otherwise they may come back to bite you at a later date. This may mean investing more in the up-front research process, but will be extremely worthwhile in the long-term.

Validate it

You can carry out due diligence on the information and data that you have by regularly asking the recipient of that data to confirm certain aspects of it. Ask them if this is their email address, phone number and whether they are still interested in receiving certain information that you are offering. Of course, many won't even reply at all and others will tell you to delete their data. All par for the course and part of the validation process - but it is making the information you *are* left with even more valuable.

When it comes to procuring - often at very high expense - information or raw data for business purposes, you really do have to go one step further. This will mean requesting sample information from the potential supplier and qualifying the data supplied by using other sources of knowledge. This could include talking to people on the ground with local market or relevant category knowledge, comparing information with other, less-detailed, 'free' sources - or contacting existing customers of the supplier to obtain testimonials.

Combine and consolidate it

Individual pieces of information and data will have their own discreet value, but multiple levels of value can be extracted when you sort and segment the information you have into *similar areas of relevance*. By bringing information together, you can begin to see the bigger picture. This can often lead to a Eureka! moment when, for example, you identify a common thread or insight that runs across all the information which you have invested your time and energy in managing.

When carrying out this exercise, remember to look closely at all the information sources you have; *each* may have a relevant insight. This should also include combining information with other secondary sources such as books, the Internet, CDs, DVDs, seminars and workshops notes or handouts that you may have obtained.

Present it professionally

So now you have all your information sorted, segmented; you are clear as to what it all means! The next stage is to *do something with it* to continue the value extraction process. Whether it is a hobby or a business project that you are working on, this next stage is of critical importance and one that you as the Information Overlord will need to excel in.

Presenting information can take on many forms; it does not (necessarily) mean standing up and sharing what you have learnt with friends, colleagues or business partners. (This might, however, be one of your goals; later in this book I will provide some useful tips on how to effectively share information as a speaker with audiences large and small.)

The first thing to remember is to Keep It Simple (KIS). All of the detailed 'stuff' you have collected and assimilated needs to be honed down to the most salient points. Yes, you can retain all of the data, but only include it within the appendices section of your report or as a post-presentation handout. Generally people will not want to read through, or listen to, all the numbers or correspondence that you may have used to reach the conclusions you have.

> Information delivers real value when the recipient makes a decision or carries out an action as a consequence of the insight they have gained by having it shared with them in a professional manner.

The task of the Information Overlord is to present the key learning from information in such a way that it *attracts attention from the individual reader or audience.*

Use pictures, pictograms, key words and key numbers - keep 'granular' detail to a minimum, wherever possible. By presenting the information that you have in a way that is more readable, workable and deliverable can significantly increase the value it has.

Lastly, remember to deliver your information presentation in different formats. If you are not supplying your presentation in paper or book format and are relying on the recipient to read it on their computer, you will need to consider converting it to, for example, PDF format. (Check out *www.adobe.com* if you don't know much about this very useful way of sharing information with people around the world.) Video presentations on, e.g. *www.youtube.com* have been a growing way for people to share knowledge. And although this may be 'free' to users, it helps establish your knowledge as valuable and bona fide; if you have good material, users will beat a path to your door to access it.

Customise it

Different people will want information delivered in different ways. At a personal level, friends and family members may want to know lots of detail, see lots of pictures of where you have been on holiday etc. The business analyst will want to see reams of information and data so that he or she can carry out the job of analysing, looking for trends and business opportunities. The Chief Executive Officer in the boardroom, however, will want to see the key learning from the information

- not the detail. Pictures and words often do the job here - but make sure you have the data to hand, should a question arise during your presentation!

> Customising to meet the needs of the end recipient or customer is essential in order to extract maximum value from information and data.

Including the right information tripled the response

A young entrepreneur recently placed an advertisement in a national newspaper after putting a lot of thought into the copy. It worked reasonably well, although it just had a website address for people to make contact. However, after I suggested he add his full street address, an email address, a mobile phone number for out-of-hour calls, some social media links and a QR (quick response) code, the response tripled.

New incognito window

Everywhere we go on the Web, we leave a trail behind that might sometimes be undesired - and sometimes serves us well.

We all like it when the waiter or the shop assistant knows and serves us with what we want and the way we want it. We tend to visit, more regularly, the places where we are already known and this process tends to apply to many other areas of our lives. The online service providers know this and, as a consequence, collect information about our behaviour, habits and preferences. The next time we visit them we are given the opportunity to buy what we like most or what they think we will like most. And that is great, isn't it?

But what if you don't want to leave any traces of information or be identified? You should simply switch to the *anonymous mode* that is available in most browsers. When you open your browser in the 'incognito mode', all the tracking and user identification and other information is, by default, disabled (as much as it can be); you only receive generic, up-to-date results. In Google Chrome it's called 'New incognito window' and in Internet Explorer, 'InPrivate Browsing'.

Explain it carefully and properly

I was in a meeting with some clients recently who sell marketing services into medium-sized companies. They were telling me that they are often amazed as to the number of marketing managers that they come across who have "absolutely NO idea about social media and digital marketing"; in many cases they are distrustful of it and even, in some instances, scared of it. My client was explaining that their strength was carefully explaining about the information services that they had to offer. Many times, after hearing this, the marketing manager client would then agree a digital activity programme, perhaps starting with a pilot LinkedIn campaign; were it to prove successful, it could be rolled out into other social media channels including Twitter, Facebook and YouTube for video marketing.

The Information Overlord knows that information becomes powerful and more valuable when people *really* understand it.

Allow access and manipulation

Remember back to when Bloomberg first allowed subscribers to generate analytical graphs and other kinds of models, using real-time market data, this proved to be an invaluable service to the wider Bloomberg community. Think along the lines of adding services that make better use of the raw information materials that you offer or buy.

Transform raw information into knowledge

It's what high-end editorial products such as newspapers and specialist newsletters have been doing for years. Make information useable, user friendly, bigger and better, simpler by adding context, vision and a new perspective.

Self-assessment tools

By continually analysing, thinking and asking questions - and by being your own severest critic - you start to think about information in a totally different way. Most people don't. They just take things for granted and accept things as they are. Self-assessment is an ongoing process and is a major weapon in the armament of the Information Overlord.

- Is the information the best it can be?

- Is the information the most user-friendly it can be?

- Can I get it any quicker?

- What can I plan and implement to take advantage of the information?

Moving from marketplace to marketspace

In the good old days, it was relatively easy to actually see how much stock you had on the shelves or in the warehouse, or how many customers moving in and out and hopefully buying. These days we tend to operate in a more virtual world; sales happen in the Internet space and much of the product movement is outsourced, so we do not see so many physical goods or sales activity.

As we move further and deeper into 'marketspace', and further away from marketplace, we depend more and more upon 'value-added' information to tell us what is happening, where and when, in every stage of our business and even our personal lives. Just think about how you track your mother's birthday gift order progress on Amazon.

Back to basics

In the late 1960s and early 1970s I owned a mini-empire consisting of seven motorcycle shops, two furniture shops, a forty-bedroom hotel and a small mail order business. They were rapidly spiralling out of control. Fortuitously for me, I met an affable old Irishman by the name of Seamus O'Rourke, who ended up being my first business mentor. Within days of Seamus coming on board, he had organised things such that every shop was a profit centre in its own right; and every single day, without fail, each manager had filled in an A4 sheet of paper, detailing sales, cost of sales, overheads and cash on hand. Within seconds of viewing that information you could see who was doing what, who was making or losing money and where to put the emphasis to turn any given situation around - instantly.

The moral of the story: what is called for now, right now, is back-to-basics information that can be assimilated in seconds within the blink of an eye.

When less is more

The problem these days: it is so easy to generate volumes of information, so much so, that no one has enough hours in the day to read and assimilate it, let alone implement it. Serious work and effort is needed to discover the minimum amount of accurate information that is required to create maximum results. I remember an old sales manager who I worked with; he composed a beautiful sales letter that actually accomplished everything we wanted it to. It was short, concise and got results. It made me laugh when he said, "If I had more time, it would be even shorter!" He clearly had the makings of an Information Overlord.

Information Technology

I am ever-mindful that, as well as creating billions upon billions of dollars, 'IT' has also cost some companies billions of dollars.

Most Information Technology projects seem to go over budget - or at least we never seem to hear about those that do not. How often is the *real* cost of ownership properly calculated before a new project is progressed? How often is the 'do nothing' option properly considered in the go/no go equation? How often are the additional tasks that have to be carried out to maintain the new system considered within the five-year return on investment plan?

There is a belief that if a computerised, electronic process is put in place to replace an offline information management process, it will always be better for the individual or the business, delivering cost savings or additional revenue. The Internet has clearly delivered on this premise and continues to add real value to people's lives. Harnessing the power of the Net should now be a prerequisite for any new IT project as it will add significant economies, particularly for the individual operator or small- to medium-sized business.

Secure it

Securing information - particularly if highly valuable - is essential, but it does cost money.

At the lower end of the scale, at home or in the small office, you might backup all your information on an external hard drive; at the other end of the scale, your data can all be stored in an underground vault, hundreds of miles away from your company's headquarters. Should disaster strike, all data is preserved. Scenarios beyond anyone's worst-case scenario came with the 9/11 attack on information power houses that we witnessed with horror at the World Trade Center in 2001, and with the 2011 Japanese earthquake and tsunami.

These days you can download vast amounts of simple data onto a memory stick within minutes. It doesn't take too much imagination to grasp how a disgruntled employee may very quickly download all of your data, (and I do mean all of it) and walk calmly out of your building, without a care in the world - to read it, use it or sell it, as he or she sees fit, at a later date.

Securing information can be expensive, sometimes disproportionally so, to the value of the data that you are aiming to secure. Often, however, it only requires putting a few simple steps in place and using relatively low-cost hardware or software to make a noticeable step change in the security level of your information. Most importantly however, it is all about *people processes* - yes, the ones that have to flip the switch, put in the USB stick, abide by the company data security processes and their individual employment contracts. It is vital that, within business, the HR Manager take an active role in the security of company data and information. At home, this role may, of course, fall to the parent or guardian!

The place of universities in the information value chain

It's time universities stopped asking people to *memorise* things, and instead started teaching them how to *find* the information - and how to *manage* it. At the very least, there could be an extra subject on the curriculum dedicated to managing information. However, many would argue that the whole approach to teaching needs to be completely overhauled and changed to make it relevant to current times.

Social Media

'Social Media' - the latest buzz word for sharing information about yourself, your life, your work and leisure.

As well as individuals sharing personal information, companies large and small are now using social media to get the message across about their products and brands; many see it as the Holy Grail to engaging with their consumers. Whilst this in many ways is true, there can also be downsides to entrusting your information to social media channels. Once it has been 'uploaded' it can be there for many months - or even years. It is imperative that adequate steps are taken to share only the information you want other people to see, otherwise you may have to undertake a costly reputation management exercise to clean up the trail you have left behind.

The following are currently the most popular social media platforms being used to share information today:

LinkedIn

Designed for professionals who want to share their skills, expertise and experience with the wider business community. Also a great place to seek new career opportunities.

A few words of advice though. The majority of people, in my experience, do not add value to the information that they put into their LinkedIn profile. This is such an important exposure for you that it is well worth the effort of spending a week or two, maybe even with the help of another person or your team, to work out the exact information and profile you want to create to elicit the response you desire, from the type of people you want to hear from.

Twitter

From what I see day-to-day, Twitter has become the mouthpiece of choice for celebrities, politicians and the clergy. Rarely a day goes by without something appearing in the press that has emanated from Twitter dialogue - often resulting in the downfall of the individuals involved.

My advice to you, as Information Overlord, is to tread carefully with the information you share, should you decide to open a Twitter account. It can be a real boon, of course, if you want to share your thoughts in a constructive manner on current topics or the business space that you might work within with a worldwide audience.

Facebook

Now boasting over 900 million subscribers - that's nearly one sixth of the world's population - Facebook is clearly the biggest social media channel out there today. A few other key statistics worth remembering:

- Nearly 50% of active users log onto Facebook every day
- The average user has 130 'friends'
- The average user is connected to over 80 community pages, groups and events
- On average, more than 250 million photos are uploaded daily
- More than 70 languages are available on the site
- More than 75% of users are outside the USA
- More than 350 million active users access Facebook via their mobile device

"Wow!" I hear you say! This is great news if I have information with value to share. Just remember, though, you will not be popular with a large number of people if you upload irrelevant, non-added-value drivel. Keep it simple, interesting -

and relevant to the audience you want to 'present' to. And remember, as the Information Overlord, not to share personal or confidential business information that could get into the wrong hands.

YouTube

Information in video format is fast becoming the media of choice for many people around the world who are finding ingenious ways of using it to gain value - in hard cash terms - by sharing the knowledge and skills they have. Video brings information to life in a way that few other media can compete with, often transcending language barriers.

With the advances made recently in technology, it is now cheaper and easier than ever to create your own high-quality video, upload it to YouTube and watch the viewer numbers roll in. Remember though, it's the content that really matters. Whatever you share has to provide value in an easy - and preferably entertaining - way for the viewer to digest. And again, drivel will only get you noticed for all the wrong reasons!

ZOOM SECRETS

Your Personal Action Plan (3)

1. **Realise the value of research**

   Research is one of marketing's most powerful, yet underutilised tools. It is a hidden secret, if there ever was one.

   There are numerous ways of conducting research. When it comes to business, it can be as simple as questions being asked of consumers in the street, through to using consumer focus groups, online desktop research and questionnaires being mailed through the post.

   Think about and list which methodologies would work for your organisation or department to unlock potential value from new ideas or knowledge already present within the people and resources of your business.

   a.

   b.

   c.

2. **When using or presenting information, validate it first**

When it comes to procuring information or raw data for business purposes, you really do have to go one step further to validate it. This will mean requesting sample information from the potential supplier and qualifying the data supplied by using other sources of knowledge.

Think about the key information resources that you use in business and list the methods used to validate each of them.

1.

2.

3.

4.

5.

3. Consolidate multiple sources of information

Individual pieces of information and data will have their own discreet value, but multiple levels of value can be extracted when you sort and segment the information you have into similar areas of relevance.

When carrying out this exercise, remember to look closely at all the information sources you have; each may have a relevant insight.

List below five of your key information sources with common themes that could be brought together to create one single compelling information resource to be used for analysis and insights extraction.

1.

2.

3.

4.

5.

4. Create real value for the audience when presenting information

Information delivers real value when the recipient makes a decision or carries out an action as a consequence of the insight they have gained by having it shared with them in a professional manner.

Presenting to your boss or senior manager can be a daunting task. You need to take time to prepare a concise, audience focused, simple presentation that gets across the key messages that you want to impart in a succinct manner.

What help do you need to achieve this? Identify three key areas that you believe you need to develop and then ask a friend or colleague who is good at presenting to share some tips. If your company offers training, take up the opportunity as soon as possible.

1.

2.

3.

5. Transform raw information into knowledge

It's what high-end editorial products such as newspapers and specialist newsletters have been doing for years. Make information useable, user friendly, bigger and better, simpler by adding context, vision and a new perspective.

1. *Critique the reports your business or function generates - do they create interest and provide actionable insights?*

2. *Introduce simple reporting - one sheet of paper only for each report.*

CHAPTER 4

RETRIEVING INFORMATION

"The sheer relief when information is retrieved makes the effort of retrieving it worthwhile"

Ron G Holland

The only thing they wanted was 'Information'

I used to love the 1960's TV spy thriller *The Prisoner* in which Patrick McGoohan was known as Secret Agent John Drake, a.k.a. 'Danger Man' (or 'Secret Agent Man' in the States). He was a British agent at the end of his career, when he was mysteriously taken prisoner. When he asked what it was that his tortuous captors wanted, their stern reply was, "Information!" To which McGoohan dryly replied, in his distinctive accent, "You won't get it!"

It seems to me that everyone, not just the world's governments and secret services, wants to retrieve information, but how? You, of course, as the Information Overlord will have the answer, won't you?

Where is it?

Even in our small office, every day I observe people struggling to retrieve data that they've lost, can't find because it has been badly labelled or, somehow or other, has vanished into cyberspace. All of this is a major distraction, is frustrating and leads to non-productivity, downtime and loss of profit. Think about how many times this negative scenario is repeated, day in, day out, across offices and businesses, globally. And of course it can happen in the home, often leading to intense arguments across the dinner table!

Software that creates problems

I am a great believer in research; specifically asking a cross-section of people what they think about a certain product or service. My recent quest, because of this book, was to drill down on many users of Microsoft Word 2010 and quite frankly I was appalled. The majority of the people I talked to hated it. Many of them complained that it was 'too complicated' and 'too difficult to save information easily so that you could retrieve it easily'.

Many of the IT guys and more sophisticated computer users loved it, no complaints; but it didn't escape my attention when, the very next day after my survey, I heard one of them moan, "Where's my file?" Not only that, by the day's end, they still hadn't found it and stormed off in a huff when I pointed out that the software could be a whole lot simpler and more foolproof.

My wife, who is Romanian, has a lovely expression: "too clever for their own slippers", which I think sums the whole thing up in a nutshell. I really do believe these young geeks who write software nowadays are doing it for their own amusement, coding in every single option that they can think of. This is often without any consideration for the *consumer* who, (the majority I have found) only use about five to ten per cent of any given software package's functionality.

Before you read on, guess how many discrete functions buttons there could be on MS Word 2007's toolbars. Around 1,450! And how many do most users have? Maybe 200, spread over seven different tabs! And how many of them do we really know how to use... Take a moment to check out your toolbars, and see how many of the icons you can say, hand on heart, that you know what they do.

If things keep developing at the current rate it will soon be impossible for people to use what should be relatively simple everyday information management tools. What is called for is a 'back-to-basics' package that is idiot proof! The more advanced packages would be available for consumers to use as they progress up the ladder of competence.

There should be back-to-basics software packages that allow you to write and create and most importantly, save information in an intuitive fashion very quickly. Yes, there should also be more sophisticated software that allows you to mess around with all the very many other extras and options - but this should only be used if *real* value is going to be added to the information you are producing and storing.

In the mid-nineties I cannot tell you how impressed I was with Bill Gates' vision and prediction of "business at the speed of thought"; but how disillusioned I am now, 17 years on, when it's frequently like watching paint dry. We have taken so many backward steps, it's no longer funny.

Employees, designers and suppliers also create retrieval problems

It's only since I became acutely aware of the problem that my hackles now rise when, for example, a designer sends a cover for a new book with the file entitled: 'Holland 7'. Then, next, 'Holland 7.1'.

Let's take a real look at a few of the files that I have received from outside suppliers, clients and others in the last week or two:

- 'Holland invoice'

- 'advert copy #1'

- '!phone old'

- 'RGH first rough draft'

- 'ccc'

- '01 part 2'

- 'RH plus'

- 'VDB business plan #3'.

I am sure you get the point. Probably at the time of writing, those file titles meant something to the creator and, at the time of receiving the file, they may very well have meant something to the recipient. Perhaps.

But you get my drift? In an office of nine staff, this creates absolute mayhem and misery. And guess what, even with a slow turnover of staff, do you think any of those files will mean anything to a new employee when other staff leave or retire. In three years' time, who would ever guess that the file marked up 'ccc' contained literally thousands of ideas for increasing sales and profits in the mail order division. You'd never believe the file marked up '01 part 2' contained a database of the names and addresses of 40,000 of the richest people in the UK, including names, addresses and telephone numbers. 'RH plus' was a valuable digital database of CAD-models that were used in the aerospace industry that had cost hundreds of thousands of dollars to create - indeed, engineering capital.

Imagine this problem compounded in an office of a hundred or a thousand, or a corporation with 70,000 employees with 3,000,000 distributors in 90 countries. Then multiply this by practically every company across the globe. We need to get on top of it, fast!

It's not just a software solution - it's also an *education* solution

When engaging new employees, designers or suppliers, you need to make it very clear how you want files labelled before you even start. This way they will get used to marking up files so that they can be easily retrieved 'intuitively', long after the creator of the file has been buried and long after the file itself has been buried!

As well as intuitive labelling, there is a massive education exercise needed in terms of where and how those important files should be stored for future access.

Let's consider here the analogy of the purchase of a new wardrobe and the demand for an additional one terabyte network server to store information by the marketing team of a large multinational.

One partner says to the other, "I need a larger wardrobe to store all of my new clothes and shoes". In response, the other partner asks why some of the older clothes cannot be thrown out or taken to the charity shop, to free up space in the existing wardrobe. "Because I might need them sometime in the future" is the reply - so the new wardrobe is ordered!

The same scenario is often put forward as the rationale for hard disk and network server upgrades; only the 'clothes' and 'shoes' are now huge numbers of badly labelled information files of all types and sizes. The marketing team of the multi-national claim that they *might* need to access the files -

which were created five years ago - in the future and therefore the IT team must purchase a new server or storage space, be it either local or in the 'Cloud', to accommodate their request. In most instances, and to keep people happy, IT will either buy the new server or provide a hard disk upgrade. In large environments more complex storage systems are used (they are known as SAN or NAS). Just to give you some extra information, a server is not really used for storing, though it can be. A *server* is a machine with a function on a network (to serve one or more applications), while *storage* facilities are used to store information. They can usually be hard drives, and sometimes tapes, used especially for backup.

The ever-decreasing cost of IT storage space is in part to blame here. It is very easy now to buy or lease vast levels of hard disk space - whether physically or in the 'Cloud'. If this continues, we will all sink in data and information - and if technology should, one day, fail, all of our valuable knowledge could be lost in a second. People need to be trained in the art of archiving and securely backing up information - and the good thing is that technology provides many excellent solutions here to help even the most basic computer user. This will significantly reduce the risk of data loss and, more importantly, reduce the amount of hard disk or server space needed both at home and in the business environment. Throwing data out or taking it to the charity shop is clearly not a practical solution, unlike clothes in a creaking wardrobe!

The problem is so endemic I had to create Holland's Law

When software doesn't work or is too complicated for the average consumer or user to solve simple problems, Holland's Law simply states: that when a problem gets so bad, someone, preferably a layman like me, has to stand up and shout out: "The emperor has no clothes - this is not working, simply because you have made it just too complicated for the average consumer."

I am not just referring to the retrieval of information, but everything to do in connection with information.

Where is it, did we have it in the first place, shall we create it again?

There will always come a time when, in our search for a missing file, that you will inevitably say, "I don't know where it is so we need to create it again." Time is money and often the pressure is on. 'Just get the job done' is the mantra (usually expressed more forcibly!). Create a database, buy another copy of the software, re-image the logo or rewrite the business plan or sales proposal. As the Information Overlord will know, this scenario can lead to significant duplication on time and costs, whether it is at home or in the office environment.

The example of the research or marketing manager who leaves the business, having spent £500k on a recent consumer study, only to store a single copy on his PC - a PC that was cleared from his desk when he left, is only too common a case of how businesses around the world lose valuable assets that result in work having to be re-commissioned at vast expense.

Employee education and rigorous storage, labelling and indexing processes may sound boring and, in the short-term, seem unproductive, but they are essential best practice activities that have to be put in place if you and other people are to gain value from information in the future.

How do I retrieve just the right information on the Web?

As of 2012, the Indexed Web contains at least 7.46 billion *pages*, and counting. Sometimes information proves to be elusive, but you're pretty sure it exists.

Here are a few concepts which I have found useful in retrieving information that I really need - to help complete a book, or perhaps a specific bit of research I am doing on behalf of a client:

1. **Define your search**

    It is important to get your mind around what you are seeking and to define it in some detail. Write down exactly what you are looking for, why you are looking for it - and also what you don't want. That will help you come up with search terms that will drill down on the 'information gold nuggets' you seek.

2. **Massively broaden your search terms if you are getting nowhere fast**

    Try every single search term you can think of, throw into the mix some search terms that seem absolutely obscure and then come back the next day and try again. Many times this simple procedure allows me to hone immediately on what I am looking for. Choose six to eight words that you have selected very carefully, not one to two like most users.

3. Get to grips with AND, AND NOT, and OR

I know you probably know this already but it's surprising what gems most people forget on a day-to-day basis. **AND** is a great tool to be used when searching because, with it, you can dramatically reduce search times for important information. For instance, the search term 'information AND adding value AND data mining AND overload' would mean that only documents containing all those search keywords would come back to you. This can be very illuminating.

On the other hand, you can use the word **OR**, which means you are more flexible in your search and you may type in 'data mining OR overload'. This too is useful in many instances. You can also tighten up searches even more, by adding **AND NOT**. This will weed out results you don't want. Biggest tip of all is to keep using and practising; get to grips with AND, AND NOT, and OR - and see where it leads you.

4. Use phrases

The penultimate trick I have for you is to use quotation marks around your keyword search terms: then *only* that information will come back to you in that exact order. For example: "information overlord" or "information search engines".

When desperate, I also use deliberate misspelling; I am invariably in awe about how many times this silly technique leads to pages upon pages of absolute gems, when the correct spelling turned up nothing. How quirky is that?

5. Use specific search engines for the job

The final trick I want to pass on is using specific search engines for particular jobs. To help create the material for this book, I drew extensively on Scopus, Ingenta, Business Source Elite Web of Science, JSTOT, Google Scholar, as well as Google. There are literally thousands of search engines out there to use; go to *www.searchenginecolossus.com*

Transferring information from one computer to another

Here are four ways to transfer information files from one computer to another; I start with what I consider to be the simplest and quickest option, which has never ever failed me, whilst from time to time, all others have.

One important word of warning though. Ensure you are running a reputable antivirus scanner to check any files that you are transferring across, particularly if they are coming from an unknown source. It would be a disaster if all of that valuable information stored on your computer were to become corrupted or, worse, your entire organisation's data on a network server!

1. The USB stick

I love USB sticks and have many of them, dozens to be precise. The biggest one currently made is the Kingston 250GB 'DataTraveller 310' which is huge. According to Sony, the capacity can go up to 2TB, which is absolutely gigantic. When using a memory stick to transfer data, all you have to do is download your files onto it from one computer and then insert it into a new or other computer where you can easily upload the data. I have never failed to be amazed at the simplicity of the methodology. This really is idiot proof! However, people do get caught out by the need to remove it elegantly. In most cases there is no problem, but if your files have not been 'closed' correctly, you could end up being unable to access the memory stick or recover anything on it!

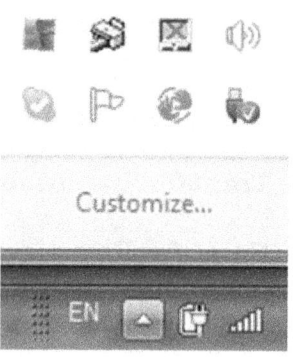

Click on the circled symbol, and wait until you get a message saying your memory stick (or external hard drive or whatever) is safe to remove.

2. Easy Transfer Cable

This is a relatively new application that now comes with most Microsoft Windows operating systems. You need an EasyTransfer cable which has a male USB connector at each end, and can be bought at most computer stores and also online for around £7 to £15. Using this method you can connect the computers together and then transfer information from one computer to another. Very nearly idiot proof!

3. Connect the hard drive manually

You can always take out the hard drive from your old computer and connect it directly to your new computer with the right cables using IDE-to-USB or SATA-to-USB connectors. All sounds so simple - but don't forget that I have enough IT guys around me to cobble dogs with and even they found it not so easy to get and make the right connections and make it all happen effortlessly. Not completely idiot proof!

4. Share over LAN

I have left this one until last because I watched my IT guys struggle with it. Although it should be relatively easy, you may have to do it many times before it becomes second nature. You'll need to enable sharing of your folders on your hard drive; go to system preferences > sharing. Then you select enable file sharing for the folder. Not recommended for the faint-hearted, layman or novice, for sure! However, if your IT people set it up for you, it should always work. That's the theory.

Sharing information over the network is now commonplace in most big businesses and a brilliant way of extracting more value from information created by one person - or perhaps a centralised function. There are now many sophisticated software tools on the market that make the job even easier - if used properly!

Data mining

Data mining is usually associated with huge mainframe computers making millions of calculations per second. However, and very simply, it is the process of retrieving and analysing data from many different perspectives and sources and turning it into useful information - or, ultimately, insights that can be used to improve knowledge, to identify new business profit opportunities or cost efficiencies.

All companies want to grow their brand loyalty and sell more products or services to existing customers; this is often the most cost-effective way of increasing turnover and profits. In the retail industry, data mining is frequently used to sift through mounds of information on what consumers are buying, on what day, and for what reason. The various loyalty card schemes enable supermarkets to do this. Typically, the process will uncover things such as *'males buy more beer on Friday afternoons'* (which might be pretty obvious) but it can also uncover esoteric facts, such as *'females buy more disposable nappies on Thursday mornings'*. This information then allows the supermarket to change prices, make special offers (to specific customers) and move point-of-sale materials around so that they tap in to their customers' shopping habits and needs.

Predictive data mining is used within the financial services industry to recognise and predict fraud within the credit card transaction arena and banking industry. It can be used for determining credit card applications and determining insurance policy rates.

Today, vast amounts of data are generated within the mail order and direct sales industries; data mining allows quick analysis of historic sales, demographics, geographic, efficiency of various sales channels and also acceptable price points.

Data mining within the oil and gas industry has been used effectively for years. This is an industry where inordinate amounts of money can be wasted on drilling unproductive wells, but the return on investment can be colossal when you strike oil or gas. Data mining can go a long way into estimating the shape of an oil field in inherently chaotic geology, giving optimum oil or gas recovery, minimising risk and maximising profits.

The Information Overlord will put aside a disproportionate amount of time to carry out data mining and analysis. Rigorous preparation is the key to many a successful outcome.

Retrieving information 24/7/365 is crucial

There is a smart piece of software that allows you to access your own computer from anywhere in the world. That's what I call a good idea. *www.gotomypc.com* Here you will discover how you may travel anywhere and still use your own computer. You are able to access all your own files, mail and network. You can do this from any browser from any computer in the world. In a nutshell, you can take your office with you, wherever you go. This leads to less frustration and more productivity, allowing you to get more done faster. Check it out.

ZOOM SECRETS

Your Personal Action Plan (4)

1. Information is only of value if it can be retrieved

Every day I observe people struggling to retrieve data that they lost, can't find because it has been badly labelled or has vanished into cyberspace. This is a major distraction that leads to non-productivity, downtime and loss of profit.

1. *Design a simple and foolproof way of naming files. Every time someone sends or saves a file that does not comply with it, make it clear that it was not complying with best practice, until everyone gets it.*

2. *Introduce file versioning in file names appropriate for your business. Usually **1.00** goes to **2.00** for major updates, **1.00** goes to **1.10** for minor updates and **1.00** goes to **1.01** for tiny updates, etc.*

3. *Be strict about enforcing file naming and versioning in the whole company until it becomes a norm.*

4. *Appoint one person to be responsible for creating intelligent folder structures, including archive folders or mechanisms to clear the folders of all older versions.*

5. *Research Shadow Copy technologies to help with file versioning, backup and retrieval. Your IT personnel will explain it to you in more detail.*

6. *Invest into educating employees how to organise, name and save files and folders - this investment will pay off in a very short time.*

2. Software is only part of the solution

When software doesn't work or is too complicated for the average user to solve simple problems, Holland's Law simply states: that when a problem gets so bad, someone, has to stand up and shout out: "The emperor has no clothes - this is not working, simply because you have made it just too complicated for the average consumer."

1. *Whatever system you put in place, make sure it's simple enough for everyone to understand - scrap it otherwise.*

2. *Evaluate the software that you use - does it actually help or create more problems than it solves?*

3. *Look very carefully at the business processes that work alongside the software you use - have they been streamlined and are savings actually being made?*

4. *Check out how many people in your business are fully utilising all of the software's functionality - if they are not, consider moving to a less costly solution.*

3. **Effective sharing of information adds value and saves time and money**

Sharing information over the network is now commonplace in most big businesses and a brilliant way of extracting more value from information created by one person - or perhaps a centralised function. There are now many sophisticated software tools on the market that make the job even easier - if used properly!

1. *Consider implementing network data sharing, either locally or via Cloud services like DropBox, SkyDrive or Google Drive.*

2. *Carefully consider who your information will need to be shared with - do not overlook external agencies/partners that may benefit from having limited access rights.*

4. Retrieve hidden insights and value from your database investment

Data mining is the process of retrieving and analysing data from many different perspectives and sources and turning it into useful information - or, ultimately, insights that can be used to improve knowledge, to identify new business profit opportunities or cost efficiencies

1. *If you have a huge database with lots of details, harness data mining to find powerful ways to increase sales.*

2. *In what ways do you feel you might be able to combine information? Allow yourself a bit of 'brainstorming' time to consider this, and jot your thoughts below. Think on the lines of "Wouldn't it be nice if I could..."*

CHAPTER 5

THE TOWER OF BABEL

"To be articulate is to stand head and shoulders above the crowd"

Ron G Holland

It strikes me that the biblical story of the Tower of Babel plays an important part in today's modern business and the 'information age'.

Up until this point in the Bible, the whole world had one language - one common speech for all people. This was the perfect environment for effective information management! The people of the earth became skilled in construction and decided to build a city with a tower that would reach to heaven. By building the tower they wanted to make a name for themselves and also prevent their city from being scattered. God came to see their city and the tower they were building. He perceived their intentions, and in His infinite wisdom, He knew this "stairway to heaven" would only lead the people away from God. He noted the powerful force within their unity of purpose. As a result, God confused their language, causing them to speak different languages so they would not understand each other. By doing this, God thwarted their plans - and I think, perhaps, in a similar fashion He may well be trying to thwart the growth of modern business.

As a communicator I often view with dismay what I see in business today. I perceive that, on a global basis, billions of dollars are being misdirected, squandered, lost, abused or not used optimally, simply because of the miscommunication between IT people and sales, marketing and management personnel. I observe that this huge gap in communication exists in the majority of modern businesses but, in reality, because it is wholly man-made, it should not exist on any level at all.

Misunderstandings on a biblical scale

The following are some examples of real interfaces between, normally, IT user and IT support. The names have been suppressed to protect the innocent - and the guilty! As you read, I am sure that many of you will be quietly remembering how something similar happened to you...

The sales manager wants the database to have more fields and behave differently and the IT support team explains that the desired change cannot be implemented easily because that particular part of the program is "hard coded." The sales manager responds, "Well, if that is too hard for you to do, why can't we hire an expert to fix it?" The IT guy retorts that "hard coded" doesn't mean it is "difficult" but instead means the database is made that way, and what the sales manager is asking for is the equivalent of asking for an easier route to the top of Mount Everest.

An IT support was called because the 'Internet was not working'. When he arrived he quickly discovered that it was the *browser* (the interface on your computer to the Internet) that was not working. He went on to explain to a very receptive audience that "the Internet" was actually the multibillion dollar infrastructure of computers, routers, servers, cables and other devices that spanned the globe.

The project manager would like space on a server to install WordPress, the popular blogging software. IT has installed it, but people still can't comment because the network folk feel that allowing the general public to post comments is a security risk; not only that, they can't understand why management would want customers to comment anyway.

A computer user called IT support because she couldn't get a VPN connection (Virtual Private Network). When the IT guy asked her if she was connected to the Internet, she said she needed the VPN connection first. After a brief argument, and when the IT guy failed to convince her that she needed the Internet connection first, she decided she'd get someone else to sort it.

A Marketing Manager wanted to share his work for comments with his colleagues around the world, but not by sending out multiple copies on email. On contacting IT, he was told that this could not be done as the company network was yet to be globally activated. If he wanted this to happen, the Marketing Manager would need to put in a formal written proposal to support the expansion of the network or to purchase specific software that would enable centralised work sharing.

A business manager was given his shiny new laptop after having been stuck with a dinosaur desktop PC from the day he joined the business. Being a very proactive person, he asked the IT guy who delivered the new laptop if his new machine came with an instruction manual that he could use, rather than having to regularly call the IT help desk for support. He was told that manuals were not provided as no one ever asked for them and that the IT team were always there to help - as long as, for each request, he logged a formal helpdesk call.

A librarian wanted to create an online record of all the books held within his library, using the software that had been on his PC for the last few years. On trying to use the software to carry out the task, he found out that it needed to be upgraded to a newer version, so immediately contacted the IT department for help. When the IT support guy arrived, he said that because the software was no longer on his list of supported products, the librarian would have to put in a formal proposal for the purchase of a new more expensive software package, before he could begin his work.

What is needed is a machine code

Computer language is binary, and it is written in 0s and 1s representing 'on' and 'off' states of an electric circuit. It can look like this 1110011000001110011111000 - this is referred to as machine code. Of course, no human being is capable of writing anything in machine code (except for a very simple code), therefore programming languages have been created, only after a program/application is written in a programming language is it converted into binary code. Those programming languages have many titles; Pascal, PEARL, Ruby, Python, C++ and many more. Some of them are so vast and complex that they have been converted in the whole programming environments - don't even ask me what that means ☺. Note the fact that there are over 8,000 programming languages and only 6,000 human languages. Like all great things that actually work, simplicity is the key. What follows is simple 'machine code' that allows IT people to communicate with sales, marketing and managers and vice-versa, ultimately helping sort out information confusion - and provides another step towards helping you become an INFORMATION OVERLORD.

When the factions communicate...

The main thing here is to slow down, stop being egotistical insofar as "my job is better than your job" or "I am cleverer than you". Take time to hold hands, share knowledge and wisdom and each other's way of doing things. Learn that both parties need each other in equal amounts - so develop a liking, trust and respect for each other. There are no sides here; everyone is involved in the same project, all fighting the same battle.

Understand the fundamentals of each other's business

By taking just a few of the other fellow's training courses can lead to a greater understanding of the terminology, the problems involved and various ways of overcoming them. Of course what I hope comes out of this book is that many more courses, both internal and external, will be developed and used to bring IT together with sales, marketing and management.

Good communication leads to increased sales

When people really communicate with each other, sales increase, information flows more effectively, the working environment becomes happier and more productive. Importantly, communicate face-to-face or by telephone wherever possible: avoid relying on bland email.

Stick some posters on the walls

Simple signs on the wall about 'good communication increases productivity' and 'listen to each other' or 'have mutual respect' can have a positive effect, especially when used in conjunction with a raft of other ideas. Try a suggestion box

- it can be anonymous, if you want, but get feedback coming in on how to communicate better - from staff, suppliers and customers!

Have regular meet ups and discussions

Meet around the water cooler or over coffee or for lunch. Take time out to let each other's lingo rub off on each other in a friendly environment that is conducive to learning.

TIPS FOR SALES, MARKETING AND MANAGEMENT PEOPLE

Learn the lingo

Try to learn IT lingo or 'geek speak' so at least you can better communicate. Buy a book on the language or pal up an IT guy to show you the ropes.

Write the problem down before you report it

A good habit to get into is to write down any error message you received and the sequence of events that led to that error message being displayed, and only then report it. It is particularly useful if you can make the problem occur over and over again, so when IT support arrives you can show them exactly what error is occurring. All too often, when IT support arrives the 'problem' has cured itself or just will not repeat when they are there.

In Windows, take some screenshots (press the 'Print Screen' key and then paste (CTL-V) into a blank word or notepad document) or copy the message (CTRL + C) and paste it in an email to the IT department. So often IT guys hear someone say "My computer is not working" and when they ask what is exactly happening, they answer "I don't remember" or "I'm not sure". This is similar to calling your car mechanic and saying "My car would not start" when you cannot (or don't) report whether you used the right car key or whether you used it at all. Give them something to work with - don't ask them to rebuild your computer from scratch just because you did not plug in the power cable!

Don't let ego, embarrassment or pride get in the way

All too often people tend to talk in jargon or 'geek speak' or 'IT speak' just to impress those around them. Unfortunately, this is not helpful to colleagues who may not have a clue what they are talking about. Ask the IT man to slow down and explain things in layman's terms - two or three times if necessary.

Reboot

Learn to re-boot your computer *before* you call IT support, because this is the second thing he'll do to get you sorted. Best bet is to switch off your computer and allow it a little time to do 'its thinking' and unravel itself and sort itself out. Make yourself a coffee or check your texts or emails on your smartphone if you haven't already done so.

Loose wires

The first thing IT will probably do is to check all cabling and wiring and fuses to make sure nothing has inadvertently come adrift - as it frequently does. Start with the habit of getting sharper; every day, make an effort toward getting cables and wiring neater, sharper and tidier knowing that this is a major problem area that, in most cases, can be avoided.

This might sound weird, but people who tend to look after their computers and treat them with respect, usually have fewer IT issues, and if there are some, they are less severe. Clean your computer's case, keyboard and your monitor regularly, and tidy the cables. Pay attention to your IT hardware, and it will save you lots of stress. You will have more confidence talking to IT guys, who will appreciate your readiness and the fact that you have covered all the basics; it will also make you relaxed, as you will know you have done your bit.

Back it up

These days computers are so reliable you get lulled into a false sense of security that all is well. As an author, I know this one only too well; crashes always seem to happen when you're at least halfway through your latest book and you lose everything and have to start again. This frustration has happened to me on more than one occasion and it can and will happen to you. Remember where you heard it first. Don't let it be necessary for the IT guy to have to communicate it to you. Safeguard that valuable information.

HELP

Before you shout for help, try the built-in help which is present in the majority of modern programs. Usually (certainly in Microsoft programs), pressing the F1 key will enable it - and often in a context-sensitive way, so the options will directly relate to the sort of problems you may be encountering. Otherwise, usually top-right on your title bar, you'll find a 'question mark' symbol - click this and help is on the way! Of course, learning how to phrase your request for help is another matter.

RTFM

How do IT guys manage to get products, computers, printers and other devices up and running? It is not some magical talent or years of studies they did, as some people think. They simply RTFM, which means, Read the Fecking Manual, of course! And you can, too.

Cleanliness is next to godliness

If you can keep your mouse clean and gently vacuum around the grilles of your computer, and your keyboard, once a month *before* problems arise, you'll keep on the right side of the IT guys. And if you know what you are doing, vacuum the insides of your computer - just be gentle, so that you don't knock anything or unplug any cables. Treat your equipment like the precision instrument that it is. If you make sure you keep all your files in a clean and logical fashion and order, you'll do the same with your desktop too, right?

Check that it's OK to log into remote support

You may have a great idea that you can log into an external remote support but this tactic is not without its dangers. It may well be best to check with IT support to see if they have any reason to oppose this move.

TIPS FOR IT GUYS, NERDS, PROGRAMMERS AND WEBMASTERS

In business, the bottom line is still King

It is the sales guys, then the marketing guys and then the managers who are at the coal face, making sales and making business happen. Try to make it easier for those guys, who are often under tremendous pressure to perform. You can do this in many ways. Try to be a better listener, talker and explainer. Try to help people understand what is happening in the business by describing things in layman's terms.

Try to understand the company objectives, in terms of sales and performance

The current economic climate leaves little room for wasted time or money. I am frequently left amazed at how little the IT guys know about the business they are operating in - almost as though they are completely disconnected from it, operating in their own bubble. Every IT manoeuvre needs to be designed around the sales, profitability, productivity, cost management, and growth of the organisation. You need to continually think in "hard numbers" and, by doing this, you realise that you are an extremely valuable cog in the big machine; your efforts are highly valuable to the overall programme.

Understanding and articulating metrics is crucial

Now is the time to study your own craft, get on top of it, and be able to assimilate the metrics yourself in such a manner you can explain them articulately to the sales, marketing and management teams. Explain exactly what you have done to increase hits, sales, traffic, stickability, enquiries or returns. Did you have more JVs, a bigger budget on Pay-Per-Click (PPC), some PR in the national press or did marketing come up with a TV campaign that blew everyone's socks off? Where did the traffic come from? How much did it cost? What was the conversion? Get to grips with exactly what is affecting the metrics, both on a positive and negative level; then discuss those metrics in depth with the team and await some feedback. Don't expect the team to be able to read those metrics and second guess what tweaking you did to create them.

Enlist teaching champions

When you recognise someone in the IT team who is really good at communicating to the 'civilians', lock onto him; get him to teach those skills and techniques to other IT guys.

A lot of communication can be non-verbal

You can accomplish a great deal by drawing or showing appropriate diagrams in manuals - or actually demonstrating a process on the computer screen, not once but several times, until the recipient has grasped what you are saying.

Good communication doesn't happen by accident

I believe that most IT people can learn a lot from sales people when it comes to information communication, especially when it comes to establishing rapport. Top-flight salesmen establish rapport with their clients by entering their 'inner world'; by becoming like that client. In simple terms, they mirror and pace the client at every conceivable level.

If the client drinks orange juice, the salesman will order an orange juice too. If the client talks about football, the salesman will join in the conversation and talk about football too. He won't break rapport by talking about motor racing, unless the client talks about motor racing. If the client talks slowly, the salesman will talk slowly; if he talks quickly, the salesman will match that pace. If the client breathes slowly, the salesman will mirror and pace that behaviour too, alongside every other behaviour the client proffers.

Once the salesman has entered the client's 'inner world' he will be able to lead, explain and educate in a way that the client is very appreciative of and receptive to.

Trying to understand and fathom out information that has not been simplified and articulated is one of today's major problems. It's one we need to get on top of. Because it's wholly man-made, we can.

ZOOM SECRETS

Your Personal Action Plan (5)

We all need to speak the same language

On a global basis, billions of dollars are being misdirected, squandered, lost, abused or not used optimally, simply because of the miscommunication between IT people and sales, marketing and management personnel.

1. *Get an IT guy to train your employees on computer vocabulary, such as the Internet, browser, caching, router, database, server, Ethernet, Windows. Sort out a basic timetable for this - who will do the training; to whom; when?*

2. *Train your employees to understand how the IT infrastructure works, how they can use it to their advantage - and how they might inadvertently abuse it. Most of them will take this information on board and increase their productivity. Again, draft an outline plan for this - who, when, to whom, where?*

3. *Brief your IT guys on how the IT infrastructure helps the business. Help them understand the business objectives, so they can focus on increasing the profits, not just upgrading the IT infrastructure, only because they would like new toys to play with. Who, when, to whom?*

4. Be brave enough to admit that you don't understand what the other person is saying. Most people don't know what the Internet is and, funnily enough, they are sure they do. Do you? Look it up and ask 10 people - you will find out that they have no clue.

5. Learn to read manuals or the 'help' screens - often, the answer is seconds away. Build in a 'licensed playtime' to your working routine: encourage staff to record particular issues or requirements - such as how to use tabs in Word; how to use pivot tables in Excel. And then once a month allow all staff to have, say, 30 minutes to 'play' with the program, help screen and manuals to learn how to carry the function out.

6. Build a rapport with a client to increase sales. Learn to mimic in a subtle way your client's behaviour, way of speaking, etc.

7. Regularly go to self-development courses to improve your listening, communication and other interpersonal skills.

CHAPTER 6

DISSEMINATION OF INFORMATION

"Share information before your competitor does - publish or perish"

Ron G Holland

'To disseminate' means to spread or broadcast a message, get the word out, sow the seed. In this chapter, we look at a few ways of doing just that, so that you, as the Information Overlord, are able to target just the right level and type of information you want to get to your target: potential clients, investors, recruitment agency in trays, whatever...

Before we do that, I thought we'd quickly look at just a few snippets of how information has been disseminated throughout the years. These days we tend to think in terms of getting out vast amounts of information into the global marketplace within seconds, but it hasn't always been like that. Many times, information disseminated was just a single message, one book or one document. There was the town crier with his big hat and bright costume, shouting out up-to-date information around the city streets and clanging his bell to attract attention. In 1440, Gutenberg invented the first printing press; this made mass production of books possible and provided the catalyst for printed information dissemination to the ordinary person.

I love the story about how, when Spain was at war with America and of how Rowan had to deliver a message to Garcia, that he stuffed it in his oilskin pouch and rode his charge through the night, travelled by boat, traversed hostile territories and jungle for three weeks until the vital information was delivered. As a young boy, I read stories about how they used carrier pigeons during the First World War to deliver vital information. And, of course, we all know Browning's *'How They Brought The Good News From Ghent To Aix'*, don't we?

I am reminded that, in 1958, the UK post office owned thousands of little red BSA bantam motorcycles that they used to deliver all sorts of information to businesses, home owners and government officials across the UK. As lads, we used to buy these motorcycles very cheaply, tune them up to the ninth degree and run them on alcohol. Mine was the fastest for many years...

At Crystal Palace, on the outskirts of London, the men who built the massive radio mast were known as the 'fools on the hill'; many folk thought the dissemination of information through the airwaves was impossible. In August 1936, the BBC prepared for the world's first high-definition TV service from Alexandra Palace. We have come a long way, in a very short time; no doubt there is much further to go yet.

The Internet

Swathes of column inches have been written about the Internet but many miss the vital points. It is still at an embryonic stage and there are a few quantum leaps to come yet. Speed is crucial and it is not good enough that the UK broadband speed is not even in the top 10 in the world, when this country has the resources and technology to make it number one. Big business (and Big Brother) are impeding growth on an unprecedented scale.

The UK has over 84% of the population now able to access the Internet - that's over 52 million people - and they deserve a better online experience that only faster broadband services can really offer. What might surprise you is that this is a greater percentage than even the United States where less than 80% of people in that country have Internet access. Only a few countries are ahead of the UK, including the likes of Iceland where over 97% of the population are online - it must be the dark evenings!

Think of the way you take flying or cars for granted, then consider how rare and primitive those modes of transport would have been to, say, your great-grandparents. Technology is much the same. In the next 30 to 60 years, all the users of the Internet will be second- or third-generation users: they will have been brought up with it, as well as computers and handheld communication devices, and all types of computerised machine - cars, washing machines, etc. Using them will all be second nature to them.

It is also highly likely that *all* the governments of the world will be on board in a much bigger and better way, including China; new generations will be born into the world of the Internet and globalisation and it will soon become totally absurd to think that some people can have access to information and others can't. The people of some of the more controlled and restricted countries are *slowly* waking up to this fact. When this actually happens it will be a massive quantum leap. At the moment, a big proportion of players are still old codgers like me who have to work it out as we go along.

Google

Like over 300 million other users, I love Google and use it every day. YouTube is owned by Google and I see a time when many people will go to YouTube first for the information they seek. This is because they are delivered a rich media experience of video and audio, which makes the receiving of information that much more interesting and - more than often - fun. YouTube is already getting nearly half a billion unique visitors a month and is known as the world's 'second most popular search engine'.

I predict that Google may not win the long-term race for search engine supremacy unless they develop highly sophisticated voice recognition systems, which are already available on the latest Apple iPhone. It's inconceivable to believe they are not already doing this. Imagine a search where you can talk and talk, maybe even articulating quite a few paragraphs of *exactly* the type of information you are seeking - and then the search engine will drill down on just what you want. (At the time of writing, this was my predication which has now come true, at least in part.) This whole arena will keep changing for the foreseeable future; the good thing is that, as each development happens, the benefits of the Internet (and particularly Google's YouTube) as a dissemination tool grows even wider, cutting across all geographical, cultural and individual ability barriers.

Social Media

In recent years, Facebook, YouTube, Twitter and LinkedIn have become the most popular social media tools available for everyday and business users to disseminate messages across the Internet. All four continue to grow significantly, with more and more people and companies signing up every day.

My good friend Stan Barat owns over 3,000 website URLs, which include all the world time zones and all the majority of UK postcodes URLs and he makes serious money from Google 'Adsense'. He ensures his Twitter accounts keep his pages at the forefront, because Google's algorithms are always seeking fresh, accurate and the very latest information, from social media sites in particular.

Social media has become an effective way to disseminate information; it fosters genuine consumer engagement by connecting with, literally, millions of people. By integrating it into your outward communication activities, you will be able to leverage social dynamics and networks to encourage participation, conversation and community building.

A few tips on creating a 'broadcast' and using Social Media tools:

1. Think strategically - do not just push out irrelevant information that will not help you achieve your ultimate goal

2. Have a clear message and do not over-complicate things; keep it simple and remember, people will only look at your message if it creates immediate impact

3. Be clear on how much time and effort this type of activity will take

4. Direct your resources to where the people are that you want to engage with

5. Use 'low risk' social media tools first - run pilot activities before investing in a full-blown multi-media campaign

6. Remember to create 'portable' content in different formats that can be accessed via mobile technology as well as desktop computers, smart TVs etc.

7. Consider developing 'viral' information, that will create mass interest in your activities, products or services by recipients forwarding on to their friends or colleagues

8. Encourage your audience to participate and recommend your information or products to others in their circle of friends or business networks

9. Remember to analyse and evaluate your activity - so that the next round brings in even better results!

10. Participate in discussions yourself - this means regularly logging in to see what dialogue is being created following your 'broadcast'

Email

Albeit relatively 'old hat' now for many of the younger users of the Internet, email is still a powerful tool for delivering information in a cost-effective manner. However, gone are the days of 'spray and pray' advertising (not that many spam operators seem to have realised this!); these days you have to hone in on just the niche that you want to target. Here are a few pointers for creating email campaigns that actually work.

- Many individuals and companies have sent out a million emails and got a zero response. The lesson here is that *your own data* is the best data and go from there. Build your own data by designing and creating a fantastic 'wow factor' newsletter that is useful and that people really want.

- To ensure that your message really hits home, do some upfront research with some friends or a small group of people - a pilot test, really - to see if what you plan to say resonates with them. Remember one thing: unless you are tapping into a real consumer or customer need, your email will fall on deaf ears.

- Make sure you create the most powerful and unique 'subject heading' you can think of, in order to entice the recipient to open the email. Split-test subject headings to see which one works best.

- Study the metrics of every mail out: see how many people actually *opened* the email, how many *read* it and how many actually *responded*. Tweak the next mail out to increase the response rates.

- Spam filters are getting more sophisticated, so you have to work even harder not to fall foul of them. Most of this will be done by early stage due diligence, and purchasing or creating correctly targeted data - alongside developing a subject heading that will interest the target audience, but won't have words and phrases that spam filters look for.

- Try to sell your product or service in three short paragraphs. Use (quick-loading) graphics and colours to raise attention. This means creating the email in HTML Web format; when you consider you have only around two or three seconds, at most, to get your message across, it's clearly worth putting in extra effort so that your information is actually read.

Books

Within the space of a few short years, eBooks have started to overtake sales of hardcover books; if the trend increases, which it will, paperbacks will soon be redundant too - it's inevitable. As the generations change, children will be brought up with eBooks and the likes of the incredible Kindle, and sales will increase exponentially. It's no good getting sentimental and saying there's nothing like curling up in bed with a good old-fashioned hardcover book. Yes, there will always be a place for them - but that's not what today's children think at all. They are comfortable and accustomed to reading on-screen.

Kindle and other eBook readers

You'd be naive to think that these books will stay forever sixteen shades of black and white. I can't predict whether it will be three, five or ten years, but there will come a time when battery and screen technology will catch up and you will be able to read full-colour picture books on-screen without the battery going flat in less than an hour. More and more authors are using eBooks to get their information out in the most cost-effective manner to an eager buying public. This will often lead to major publication deals for the lucky few who get noticed, as their books climb the Amazon readership rankings, attracting large numbers of followers posting 'five star' comments. However, self-publishing is now even more practical than it ever was.

Libraries

More and more libraries are now making sure that they offer access to information on the Internet; those that don't will get left behind. Amazon has already announced that over 11,000 libraries in the US now offer eBooks in Kindle format. Wow! All your highlights and notes come to an end after your loan period expires and you can no longer access the book on your device - but Amazon stores your highlights and notes on their servers, should you ever borrow the book again. And now with the new Kindle Touch and Kindle tablet, any navigation and highlighting is a breeze. Clever stuff!

Public speaking

As an accomplished public speaker of over 30 years, I find it strange to hear that people have a great fear of standing up in public. Research shows that the greatest fears we have are as follows:

1. Fear of public speaking (Glossophobia)
2. Fear of death (Necrophobia)
3. Fear of spiders (Arachnophobia)
4. Fear of darkness (Achluophobia)
5. Fear of heights (Acrophobia)

Giving a lecture about dead spiders, from a high stage when the lights go out is, possibly, not the dream that many aspire to!

When I was living in the States in the early 1980s and my book *Talk & Grow Rich* was published, I suddenly found myself in great demand with networking and direct sales companies who wanted me to come and talk to and motivate their groups. I was taken off guard, as I had never spoken on stage before. I did have good information to deliver that I was passionate about, so I decided to present it to 30 empty chairs that I set up auditorium style in my living room. For a week I practised in front of that 'imaginary audience' and, at the end of it, I delivered my first public talk in Newark, New Jersey, to a bunch of network marketing guys. They loved it. I referred to 'passion' earlier - this is really important and often the one thing that will help overcome any confidence issues you may have. If you know your subject well and really believe in it, your presentation delivery will fly.

I have been a public speaker since that day in Newark, New Jersey. If you have information that you need to impart, to either large or small groups of people, and have fear of public speaking, it will have a negative effect on your career and business if you do nothing about it. Get hypnosis, practise like I did or go to Toastmasters or one of the many other public speaking academies and get it sorted. As the Information Overlord, you'll have a load of fun at the same time and be able to deliver your information in a confident, compelling and, above all, memorable fashion.

ClickBank and other purveyors of digital information products

ClickBank is the largest purveyor of digital information products on the Internet. These products range from making money, succeeding in Internet marketing, picking up girls, through to growing and selling tomatoes. All human life is there! There are thousands of digital products and ClickBank is doing over 35,000 transactions a day.

What is great about the ClickBank concept is that it provides the man on the street, as well as small to larger businesses, with the opportunity to generate an income or revenue stream very quickly from the information they want to disseminate and market. The results speak for themselves - ClickBank has paid out over $2billion in royalties to their vendors, authors and affiliates in the 10 years they have been going. This alone gives an insight into the demand for digital format information. Of course, others are jumping on the bandwagon; at time of writing, late 2012, *www.jvzoo.com*, *www.digiresults.com*, *Amazon.com* and *eBay.com* spring to mind and are worth checking out if you want to buy or sell digital information.

After your information product is sold

Our research shows that, although a huge amount of information products are bought, *a large percentage of that product is never read, viewed, listened to or acted upon.* One seller of language training audios, for example, discovered that 45% of the products he sold were never actually listened to.

Purveyors of information products should heed the advice of old master salesmen: 'follow up and follow through'. We often phone clients to make sure they have downloaded the product they have purchased and that they have actually started to listen to or read it. We use powerful, call-to-action, personal follow-up emails set up on an 'auto-responder' to re-sell the package (or updates, extensions or variants) again and to ensure that it is read and acted upon.

Sometimes, what is called for is not only the re-selling letter, which reminds the customer of all the reasons and benefits they bought the product in the first place, but also to include a short audio or booklet that loudly states: READ/LISTEN TO ME - NOW. The last thing any serious business wants is swathes of their information products ending up unread, unused - and therefore not converting that consumer into a great customer for the next five or ten years. Remember also that happy customers, who have learnt something valuable from your information products, will more than likely recommend your services to their friends – or, even better, their global networks. You get yourself a willing sales force, working for you for nothing!

Universities in the information dissemination chain

The word university is derived from the Latin *universitas magistrorum et scholarium*, which roughly means 'community of teachers and scholars'. I like to view them as a place where *information* is translated into *knowledge* that can then be converted into a *benefit* for all mankind; education, health, wealth and also for the development of businesses, products and services.

As in most things these days, we are seeing a dramatic shift as things change from 'hard copy' product to 'soft copy'. Universities and libraries will no longer just concentrate on procuring, storing and handling physical books; they will instead start concentrating on storing digital information that they can efficiently disseminate as and when it is required. The key to universities' future success will be judged, more and more, on their ability to work closely in a strategic manner with partners from the commercial world.

Universities carry out rigorous, high-quality research; we frequently advise our clients to form strategic alliances with them when we spot an establishment carrying out research in specific sectors or industries. After you have completed your due diligence and research of specific universities operating in your sector, you may consider approaching them on a number of different levels, for instance:

- Commission and collaborate in research projects of mutual interest

- Work in partnership in developing and exploiting intellectual property

- Access expertise through consultancy and services

- Assisting in new product development

- Ensure your services are operating at optimum efficiency.

Approaching reputable third-party institutions to assist you in your information dissemination strategy can reap significant rewards. The process will also add valuable qualification and credibility to your information products and services that will resonate with both your existing and potential new clients.

ZOOM SECRETS

Your Personal Action Plan (6)

1. Share out information before your competitor does

Remember that when you publish information, the recipient must get something of value from it, otherwise it will be instantly deleted and you rarely get a second chance with that person again.

Think about:

1. *Spreading your message to as many people as you can.*

2. *Harnessing free social media like YouTube, Facebook and Twitter: Think how you could penetrate the market and increase your prestige with books, eBooks, and other publications - maybe publish a free book on Kindle?*

3. *Creating a digital product and selling it on ClickBank or other online services: Brainstorm with colleagues how this could help your business and identify public institutions that might be interested in collaborating with your business.*

4. Collecting your customers' email addresses and send them regular email newsletters or follow-ups, especially right after they bought your products to offer help and make sure they actually use them.

5. Designing all your marketing campaigns with a clear business objective following sound marketing principles - don't just tweet or post an update for the sake of it.

2. Public speaking offers a unique opportunity to become a key person of influence on your information subject

If you have information that you need to impart, to either large or small groups of people, and have fear of public speaking, it will have a negative effect on your career and business if you do nothing about it.

Remember, If you know your subject well and really believe in it, your presentation delivery will fly.

Consider:

1. *Practicing your speech or presentation in front of the mirror at home.*

2. *Getting hypnosis.*

3. *Joining your local Toastmasters or one of the many other public speaking academies to raise your game.*

4. *Asking your HR manager, if you are lucky enough to have one, to put you on a public speaking/ presentation skills course.*

CHAPTER 7

INFORMATION TECHNOLOGY

"When ego led 'Information Technology' is replaced with egoless 'Business Technology' explosive growth will begin"

Ron G Holland

IT - 'Information Technology' - refers to anything related to computing technology, such as networking, hardware, software, the Internet, or the people that work with these technologies.

Most medium- to large-sized companies now have IT departments for managing computers, networks and other technical areas of their businesses. Typical IT job roles include systems analysis, computer programming, network administration, computer engineering, Web development, technical support and many other related occupations.

The scope and responsibilities of IT departments have had to rapidly adapt over time. This is not purely as a result of the exponential growth in technology, but also, for example, because of environmental change. More and more employees work from home these days, cutting office and travel costs, as well as helping to create a better work/life balance for themselves. The rapid growth in Internet connectivity and speed will have helped make this a logical choice for many people and employers - but every home-based employee will need IT support in some way. The Information Overlord will also be cognisant of the fact that the more home-based employees there are, the more challenges there are for managing disparate silos of *information.*

Over the years, everyday information-based tasks that were traditionally dealt with manually have been replaced by technology-based solutions that now have to be managed and maintained - either by ourselves or, if we are lucky enough, the IT department. Long gone are the days when you would send a handwritten note with a request on it to your boss or colleague and then have to wait for the internal mail to return it to you with their response. Do you also remember the times you had to present information to a group of people using 'acetates' and an overhead projector? I remember when computer-based presentation software was first made available to me to use for my first big presentation to a large audience. To play safe - and because I did not trust the new IT software - I still printed off a set of acetates to take with me on the day!

Clearly, information technology has moved on by leaps and bounds over the years and the level of trust we have with it now I would estimate to be pretty high. For better or worse, we all now live in the "information age" and have to manage both our personal and work lives around it. But where will it all end? Let's examine a few aspects of IT and also look at where current trends might be leading us.

Computers

Most folk seem quite content with their computers; for well under £500 you can get an all-singing all-dancing model, with a big screen, that will certainly perform most everyday personal or work information-based functions. However, when you compare the modern computer to the modern car, you'll see that computers still have a long way to go, reliability-wise. Imagine if your car behaved like your computer and every other day froze, crashed, locked you out or had to be re-started for an inexplicable reason. How would you like it if the more information your car took on board, the slower it would go? Or what if every time you bought a new car you'd have to learn all over again, because none of the controls would do what they did last time? If a new set of tyres meant changing suspension settings, or buying a new compatible set of pads. Imagine having to wait a few frustrating minutes before your car was actually ready to drive, even though the engine was running, while it was performing its start-up checks and initiating the brakes, clutch, air conditioning, lights, and so on... And if, when a new motorway was built, only cars of a certain age or engine size were able to drive on it. Computers have a long way to go, certainly, but regarding computers versus cars, I'm quite amazed that cars run at all, given all the moving parts in them!

On the other hand, computers evolve around 200 times faster than cars. Bill Gates reportedly compared the computer industry with the auto industry and stated "If GM had kept up with technology like the computer industry has, we would all be driving twenty-five dollar cars that got 1,000 miles to the gallon."

When it comes to selecting a new computer, many people do not quite know where to start. Just because I regularly use them, and seem to know how to operate one, many a friend or business contact will ask me for advice on what they should be buying to replace their creaking five-year-old model. My response will always be the same - take a pen and paper and list all of the likely needs you will want the new PC or Mac to meet.

If it is just simple information tasks, such as report writing, emailing friends and surfing the Internet, you will be able to get away with a very low-spec, low-priced machine. The minute you add a medium graphics requirements such as high-resolution photographs, videos, etc, you will need to move up the specification and price scale. And if you are a serious games player, or create or view a lot of videos, or need to send large amounts of information over the Internet on a regular basis, you'll need to move up the price scale even more. Never skimp on memory or hard disk size - they are currently very cheap, and much easier to specify when you are buying the machine rather than needing to upgrade later. This is where I have been let down the most, as every piece of new software that I installed needed more and more memory to operate at full potential. To misquote Parkinson's law, the more space you have on your new computer, the more you are likely to fill it!

The amount of information you have to transfer from your old computer to the brand spanking new one should also be carefully considered. This is the chance you have been waiting for - the opportunity to delete or archive 'stuff' that you have not had to refer to for years! Take advantage of the moment - just make sure that your new computer's hard disk is big enough to take all your old, most valuable information as well as all the new information you are likely to create in the future. You might even want to consider having two hard disks in the new machine - the additional one can then be used to back everything up, a precaution we should all take when using computers and that I will talk about later.

The latest trend in desktop computers is to have two storage drives: a very fast SSD (solid state disk) to store your OS (operating system, such as Windows 7) and documents, while moving all big files such as videos, games, photo collections to a larger HDD (hard drive disk). Once the prices of SSD drop significantly, our old HDDs will become history, it seems.

Switching them on

When it comes to switching computers on, you don't really need to see pages and pages of technical jargon. What needs to happen is exactly the same as when you switch on your television - it immediately bursts into life and you can start surfing the Net or working straight away. It makes me laugh: I keep hearing they can make a computer that can now compute 1,000 trillion instructions per second and light up a screen with 2.5 million colours - and I tell the computer guy I don't need any of that: all I want is a computer that comes to life the second I switch it on. He says, "Can't do that mate…" and I tell him to get real!

All new operating systems have a "Sleep" option that puts your computer into standby, saving a lot of electricity; it only takes two to ten seconds for the computer to 'wake up'. I often put my Windows 7 computer to sleep a few times a day, but it might be a month or more before I reboot it. It still works quite efficiently.

Switching them off

I just want to give my take on switching computers off, only because so many people ask me. The question is: should I leave my computer running all night or should I switch it off and re-boot every morning? The answer is, as I see it, 50% switch off the computer every night and 50% leave them on. At night time, you can see computers in big offices across the world, all still on, many of them with the day's work still showing and others with screen savers blinking away. It boils down to personal choice and your own organisation's policies; computers don't seem to mind, nor do I. I would suggest though that every business at least, should put in place an environmentally friendly policy that all employees abide by and that is driven by factors such as optimum power consumption - and data security.

In the old days, many companies asked their employees to leave the computers on for the night, but to log off, so that scheduled updates could take place. Nowadays, updating does not usually require that, so there's no real need to do it. Still, many people believe that to be the case and, 10 years later, they continue advising others to leave the computers on. When, though, was the last time they asked the IT department about that? Always question people asking you to leave a computer on - it certainly wastes electricity and possibly shortens your hard drive's life span. If you have a home or a standalone computer, you do need to switch it off and on (re-boot it) in order to allow some automatic software updates to take effect. And re-booting can also allow a computer to 'empty its cache' - to remove any temporary or unwanted files that it has been holding, 'just in case'; this can have quite a significant effect on your computer's performance, so is well advised.

Don't get lulled into a false sense of security - computers still crash

It surprises me how many folk, including myself, get lulled into a false sense of security because they think their computer is running reliably. The truth is that computers still crash all the time; when they do, the loss of data can cause untold disruption, sometimes for years to come. There are a couple of points to make here.

The first is to *regularly save and backup* daily on a spare internal or external hard drive or to somewhere in the 'Cloud'. Remember, too, that data loss can occur if your computer is stolen, so although an internal drive will keep your data secure, you still won't have access to it if your computer has gone! Cloud-based storage is excellent, but an external hard drive, kept apart from your computer, is also an effective way of ensuring you always have a backup copy.

The second is to *keep reminding employees to backup* because many of them don't, and it's you who will foot the bill when the timely big project has to be done all over again.

You, as the Information Overlord, will put a robust data backup process and policy in place, to safeguard all the valuable information that sits on your IT hardware.

Software

Software can probably provide the solution to any of your information management nightmares, but finding the right package and software partner to deliver your needs might be a lot harder than you think.

The problem nowadays is that most new software seems to offer limitless functionality that far exceeds the needs of the user. Coders need to stop working all through the night proving how clever they are, showing how many functions they can cram into a certain piece of software. They should get out during the day, and ask real people - in live businesses, factories and offices who have to use their products - what they really think and what they can do to make things simpler, more reliable and more intuitive. This all comes down to putting in place a robust programme of consumer research to identify important consumer needs before bringing to market a new software package.

Whether for personal or business use, here are a few Information Overlord tips to consider before investing in new software:

- Write down all of your (and other key stakeholders') likely needs - if for large-scale business use, this should be as part of a formal brief to a potential software developer or licensed partner

- Make sure you have carried out a thorough audit of the existing 'as is' manual process and that this is thoroughly documented, so that you can always refer to it at a later date

- Consider your wider home or office IT environment - what impact might this have on the software you choose - will your new package integrate with existing or legacy systems you already own and might continue to operate?

- Map out and document the ideal process that you would like the new software to automate or support

- Along the journey to your final choice, make sure that other key users of the software come on that journey with you; they are most likely to be the ones to complain if the wrong package is installed on their computer or network!

By applying these tips, you will be in a good position to consider what it is that you really need. This should ultimately lead to an investment decision based on fact and insight, rather than pure fiction or 'nice to have' functionality aspirations.

The Internet

The Internet really began with the development of computers in the 1950s with 'point-to-point' communication between mainframe computers and terminals, which then led to point-to-point connections between computers. Networks such as 'ARPANET' were developed in the 1960s and early 1970s using a variety of protocols. ARPANET, in particular, led to the development of protocols for inter-networking, where multiple separate networks could be joined together into a 'network of networks'.

Commercial internet service providers (ISPs) really only began to emerge in the late 1980s and 1990s. The catalyst to mass consumer usage came when the Internet was commercialised in 1995 when 'NSFNET' was decommissioned, removing the last restrictions on the use of the Internet to carry commercial traffic. During the 1990s, when we all began to discover the benefits that the Internet could provide, we could only access online information using horrendously slow dial-up modems - remember those days?

Since then, the Internet has had a massive impact on all of our lives and cultures and probably has a part to play in almost every aspect of our day-to-day routines, whether visibly or as part of the infrastructure hidden behind the scenes. And it was really the "invention" of the World Wide

Web that brought life to the Internet. Driven by the mass adoption of the World Wide Web, the Internet continues to grow, transmitting ever-greater amounts of information, knowledge, eCommerce, entertainment and social networking. To put this growth into perspective, by 2007 more than 97% of all telecommunicated information was carried over the Internet, compared to only one per cent in 1993.

When it comes to high-speed information transfer across the Net - the Holy Grail it seems of the ISP community - the UK could easily position itself for a global challenge. One thing would be for big organisations, such as BT and the government, to come together on an investment programme and roll out cable and fibre optics right across the UK. I'm not talking about the half-hearted effort they are making at the moment, allowing us to dwell in the dark ages, when countries such as Korea have broadband 200 times faster than ours. There is simply NO excuse. Believe me, the money and technology already exists to put the necessary infrastructure in place. It only needs men and women with courage, conviction and vision to see what needs to be done and act upon it. It needs certain characters, with iron will and strength of mind, to pull it all together.

What is needed now are leaders of men, both in the government and in the private sector, to step up to the plate in the same way as they did to help raise billions in investment and bring together men, women and materials for the 2012 Olympics. That is what is needed to roll out high-speed broadband across the UK and make us number one in the world. Then watch the economy flourish! At the rate the roll-out is going at the moment, I think there is a big danger that, by the time it is finished, the bandwidth will be woefully inadequate for streaming videos and all the other things that are hurtling down the 'Information Superhighway' at breakneck speed. Who would believe the sheer volume of traffic on the M1 and M25 is causing many people in the UK to call the motorway system the world's biggest car park - let's hope that the Internet in the UK is not headed the same way.

The emphasis has been put on the T of IT for far too long

I frequently meet people in IT who tell me that the emphasis is now swinging from the word 'Technology' to the word 'Information'. They explain to me that 'Technology' is now at the leading edge and that the 'Information' part of the equation has been left way behind. In that respect I think they are somewhat right, but overall I think they have got it wrong. What really needs to happen now is a paradigm shift, completely leapfrogging the word 'Information' and replacing it with the word 'Business'. Business Technology is what it's all about in the new millennium and that is where I would like to start with this next topic.

Business Technology, it's all so obvious

In my discussions and research and my desire to get to the bottom of things, I have come to the overwhelming conclusion that most of the people in IT see themselves in a support role. Obviously, all of that has to change; the real power of technology can be, and should be, to increase turnover and profits, massively help with innovation, slash overheads and create overall efficiencies right across the board. Of course, all of this is about education and a PR exercise. IT folk need to be trained and educated and told how they can contribute business-wise, to help grow the bottom line. They need to be educated away from a support role mentality and be shown how their roles really can help increase the profitability of the organisations they work within - they must aspire to be part of the 'A-Team'.

Techies who do perform...seriously

In a way I have been spoiled because I am in the privileged position as a business mentor and am able to delve deep inside many different businesses, every single day. One sector that seriously amazes me to the point of the cork popping out the top of my head is Internet Marketing (IM). Every day of the week I observe one-man bands pulling in tens of thousands of pounds by getting 2,000,000 visitors to their sites in a week. I'm talking here about unique visitors, not just hits. Wow! I meet IM guys on a weekly basis who send out a million emails at a time; they are getting a 20% 'open' rate and a 3% conversion - and are doing it over and over again. Clearly, they have got their information output and message spot on, and are very effectively using IT to deliver this level of result.

Some Techies have their wits about them

I've witnessed an email invitation that went out, filled an auditorium of about 450 people, and netted the 'one-man band' about £600k. The 'one-man' does this regularly - and effortlessly. Another IM guy sends out emails promoting a course on making money using social media. He promotes this at a price of £1,000 for the 12 modules, which last a year - and he delivers monthly content via a Webinar. He regularly attracts over 1,000 subscribers. That's a cool million for one promotion.

Other people use clever search engine optimisation (SEO) strategies and use copywriters to make sure that, when the massive traffic hits their sites, the conversion rate is the best it possibly could be. The guys doing this don't see themselves as IT people or support; they see themselves as marketing guys, or businessmen. Now, not everyone in your organisation on the IT side can be a marketer, but wouldn't it be great if, just once in a while, one of them said, "Here's a great idea to increase traffic to the site, reduce overheads or create more sales?"

Having a website doesn't always cut the mustard

You would not believe the number of people that I have interviewed who have been bitterly disappointed with their websites - many of them after having spent thousands of pounds, not with one but, in many instances, with two, three or four website designers. The customers were expecting not only a visible website up on the Internet, but one that actually worked! In most instances, as you would expect, they also wanted a website that would get good traffic and, in one case, one that would also generate sales *over and above* those that he was already getting in his offline business.

In most cases the website designer took on the job and delivered what he thought was required; a website. Nowhere in the 'conversation' was the thought of telling the customer that he didn't know anything about marketing; driving traffic to the site, writing copy, conversation rates, making the site sticky and supplying a BUY BUTTON that actually worked - and if pressed would actually accept payments that would lead to a shopping cart and get products or services promptly delivered. I say 'conversation' because, nine times out of ten, no written contract was supplied or even expected.

Even when the website designer decided to put up a video to get the customer to stay on the site for two minutes instead of two seconds, it still didn't increase sales because there was no specific call to action on the video: what to do next, who to call, what to buy or how to place an order. So although the metrics announce, "Ah, we now have traffic sticking on the site - for a full two minutes!" the end result of 'no increase in sales' was still the same.

The moral of the story is profound: it's based around the golden thread that runs through this whole book. The real problem facing us is one of *communication, education* and *understanding things* at a grass-roots level. How come that, after fifteen years into the Internet, so many people still assume that having a website up and running is a panacea. How come no one explained to them, that the bigger the Internet grows, the more websites arrive (at the rate of hundreds of thousands every week) and on those websites more pages appear, each and every one a competitor of yours, all fighting to grab attention, even if only for three measly seconds.

Of course, what is called for is more talking and careful articulation explaining; *"Yes, I can build you a website and yes, it will look good. Now, let me take you through a few of the options of how we can get you some paying customers for your products. We have to drive traffic to your site. I suggest we use both online and offline techniques. They all take time and money. What budget do you have for marketing? You do realise having a site on its own will not bring in customers - there's lots to do before that happens. Even when we have created a flow of traffic to your site, they may not like what they see. We have to pay particular attention to the copy and the graphics - make them hypnotic. Many times we may offer them a free gift or entice them to subscribe to a free newsletter. Did you have any ideas of your own? Or do you want me to explain in more detail some more options to you? There are hundreds of them and some are very sophisticated. Perhaps we should sit down and work out a proper offline and online marketing campaign with you, to ensure your site has the best possible chance of competing with the hundreds of millions of sites already out there in cyberspace."*

What is being screamed out for is more simple books, more educators, more teachers, more trainers. Less ego, less "the only solution is an IT solution", less "I know something you don't know".

To be a 'technology frightened' CEO is simply not good enough

Certainly most CEOs that I have met have got their minds around marketing, product development, HR *and* accountancy to the point where they can read a balance sheet and have an extremely good relationship with their Chief Finance Officer (CFO), often drawing on each other's strengths. In actual fact, it would be absurd if the CEO did not have more than just a superficial grasp of all of the above -

because surely that is what business is all about? To not understand any of the basic disciplines would mean not to know how to develop products, take them to the marketplace, sell, increase sales, increase market share, create turnover and ultimately generate excess profits.

The one weakness that occurs over and over again with many CEOs is the weakness and indeed, in many cases, the sheer fright of having anything to do with anything technical or IT related. Whereas they may shine in sales or marketing, and often do, they frequently whither on the vine when it comes to IT. Of course, all of this will change in generations to come, when all school kids get a thorough 'computer science' education and it will come as second nature to them. What I am talking about is in the previous two decades, right now, and two future decades.

The new millennium CEOs need to be a completely different animal

First and foremost, they need to grasp the paradigm shift that Information Technology is on the way out and Business Technology is not just on the way in, it is IN, already. Once they have grasped that, they have the ammunition to understand they are in complete control and need to get to grips with Business Technology at all costs. They do that by drilling down on their Chief Information Officers (CIO) and getting them to teach all the basics - even if they have to hear them 10, 15 or 20 times, until they sink in. If the CIO is not a willing player, they need to get a user friendly 'young IT turk' of between 20 to 25 who knows IT inside and backwards; there are hundreds of them. They take that 'young turk' IT apprentice under their wings and get him or her to act as a translator to the CEO and also explain additional IT 'stuff' in layman's terms until they do understand it.

On top of this the new millennium CEOs will get themselves off to courses, college and open university as well as buying all the latest mobile phones, iPads, Kindles and a host of other gadgets - and then get the 'young turk' IT apprentice to help familiarise themselves with all of them. The CEOs need to acknowledge that they need help in getting up to speed with all this IT stuff; what better to latch onto someone who already has a grip on it and is willing to pass the baton on. Don't be like the CEO that I know who went out looking for an iPad and ended up buying an eye pad for his eye!

Only then will the CEO be on a level playing field, so that when he or she talks to the CIO about Business Technology, and what he or she wants doing to increase sales, productivity and innovation and smash the overheads, they will be able to have a two-way discussion on how modern technology used in business may bring that about.

To be an 'unapproachable' CIO is definitely not good enough

In my experience many CIOs are missing a huge piece of the jigsaw puzzle because they tend to be so consumed by the technology, they often miss out on the *information* side of the formula - and certainly miss out on the *business* bit of the equation. The CIO of the new millennium needs to stop thinking support role and start thinking how he or she, too, can be a business driver and initiator working hand-in-hand with the CEO - to increase sales, increase productivity and slash overheads. Of course, to do this the CIO needs to be much more user-friendly, approachable - and stop talking at 800 miles an hour in 'geek speak, gobbledegook or IT lingo'. That is not serving anyone other than stroking their own egos.

The new millennium CIO will endeavour to establish a professional working relationship with the CEO, in the same manner the CFO has done. This means working hand-in-hand, in partnership, developing good communication skills and patience that allows him or her to explain things in a much simpler fashion to the CEO and others, so they can grasp and assimilate the information and put it to strategic, practical and profit generating use within the business.

ZOOM SECRETS

Your Personal Action Plan (7)

1. **Move the mind-set from 'Information Technology' to 'Business Technology'**

I frequently meet people in IT who tell me that the emphasis is now swinging from the word 'Technology' to the word 'Information'. They explain to me that 'Technology' is now at the leading edge and that the 'Information' part of the equation has been left way behind. 'Business Technology' is what it should all be about in the new millennium.

The real power of technology can be, and should be, to increase turnover and profits, massively help with innovation, slash overheads and create overall efficiencies right across the board.

Consider:

1. *Reviewing with your head of IT, how each piece of software within your business actually benefits the bottom line - are there aspects of that software that are not being commercially fully exploited ?*

2. *Inviting more IT people to your business meetings, with the objective of getting them to come up with ways for IT to help solve issues, create sales opportunities etc.*

3. *IT is now playing an ever-increasing marketing support role within the small business sector, driven by limited human resource - can the same be said of larger organisations that are still operating more traditionally?*

2. A website can be a major business asset if properly constructed regularly maintained and promoted

Many people still assume that having a website up and running is a panacea. However, the bigger the Internet grows, the more websites arrive (at the rate of hundreds of thousands every week) and on those websites more pages appear, each and every one a competitor of yours, all fighting to grab your potential customers attention, even if only for three measly seconds.

Take action now to make your site a commercial success:

1. *Make sure that visitors will know in just three seconds what you are about and what you expect them to do after landing on your site.*

2. *Put adequate time aside to create a proper offline and online marketing campaign to ensure your site has the best possible chance of competing with the hundreds of millions of sites already out there in cyberspace.*

3. *Allocate a realistic marketing support budget.*

4. *Pay particular attention to the copy and the graphics - make them hypnotic.*

5. Offer visitors a free gift/eBook to encourage them to subscribe to your free newsletter.

6. Monitor website traffic and pages visited - take immediate action to address poor performing content.

7. Keep up to date - regularly post fresh blog content.

3. **Up-to-date IT processes, hardware and software will boost overall productivity**

It surprises me how many folk, including myself, get lulled into a false sense of security because they think their computer is running reliably. The truth is that computers still crash all the time; when they do, the loss of data can cause untold disruption, sometimes for years to come.

1. *Consider buying a new computer or tablet instead of complaining about the speed of your old machine.*

2. *Backup things automatically to the Cloud or other safe locations.*

3. *Think well before you invest in new software and always do trials.*

4. *Be willing to ask very young people to teach you IT skills.*

CHAPTER 8

INFORMATION MANAGEMENT

"Manage the machines, don't let them manage you!"

Ron G Holland

According to Wikipedia, Information Management (IM) is the 'collection and management of information from one or more sources and the distribution of that information to one or more audiences'. This sometimes involves those who have a stake in, or a right to, that information. 'Management' means the organisation of, and control over, the structure, processing and delivery of information.

These days, the amount of information the Chief Information Officer (CIO) is responsible for storing increases at a staggering rate of 60% every two years. This data, when made available in an acceptable format, and with the key insights presented, can support a growing number of business decisions. If data continues to increase at this phenomenal rate, there will come a time when the cork will definitely pop out of the top of the CIO's head! Information *management* is a multibillion dollar industry, a vast subject and a headache that affects every single one of us at various levels on a day-to-day basis. This is probably the biggest challenge the Information Overlord faces.

However, storing so much data, with much of it often unstructured (e.g. text-based data), makes it extremely hard to find the most relevant information to support any particular business decision. *Processing* data is no longer a challenge, as information technology has helped us all here; but *providing* information - and in a timely, useable and acceptable format - is a problem. To make matters worse, the information is now stored in a variety of locations - including local data centres, personal computers and laptops and more recently, 'the Cloud'. A lot of valuable knowledge, experience and best practice know-how can be lost, simply because no one knows where to find it!

If ever there was a time to invoke Holland's Law, this was it. "The emperor has no clothes - this is not working, simply because you have made it just too complicated for the average consumer."

A few articulate theories

In his essay *'Information Interaction Design: A Unified Field Theory of Design',* Nathan Shedroff suggests that there are seven ways to organise anything:

- Alphabetically
- By number
- By location
- By category
- By time
- Randomness
- Along a continuum

In his book *Information Architects* Richard Saul Wurman talks about LATCH, which stands for Location, Alphabet, Time, Category and Hierarchy and the organisation of information.

In this chapter we will explore 'organising', which is one of the seven information processes:

- Collecting
- Organising
- Storing and retrieving
- Processing
- Analysing

- Transmitting and receiving

- Displaying

Only five to seven per cent of information is used effectively

It is estimated that only five to seven per cent of information is used effectively and that the global value of information now runs to $4.7 trillion annually. The value of information is largely an intangible asset and it is certainly the most critical of the twenty-first century. Among all corporate assets, information is the least understood and the most poorly exploited and managed.

Shaun is away in Dubai on a workshop for four days. Five hundred emails hit him in the face when he gets back to the office and he has people hammering on the door because he needs to be in various meetings. His blood pressure is set to boil - and he has yet to get home where he will find a further one hundred personal emails, from his wife and family, all wanting his attention!

Carter orders some images off the Internet and, three weeks later, orders the same images again. He doesn't even realise he has cost the company $60. Nothing - right, but in a company that has 500,000 employees in 97 countries, it's a financial nightmare that even the most diligent of auditors will never be able to bring to light. Multiply this mistake across a number of employees in different locations and you can see how the hidden cost of poor information organisation can soon add up.

During the course of the day, Mary Jane sends 30 emails to a work colleague that basically all say the same thing but each adding to or even contradicting previous emails. And the worse thing of all is that her colleague only sits a desk away from her!

Wayne has the habit of reading emails but not replying to them immediately, thinking that he will get to them later and answer them in his own time. However, more often than not, they slip through the Net and never get answered at all - until a few weeks later when the author says, "I haven't got your response to my email dated..." Only then does Wayne sit up and fire off a reply.

Email is clearly out of control

There are now over 250 billion emails sent every day. Yes, 250 billion! Many of these emails are jokes, marketing ploys, out-and-out scams, malicious pranks and junk. Others are sent with a view to extort money or spread viruses. Many that come from business could be better written. No wonder most executives feel absolutely exhausted by the time they get home. Stress is causing corporations billions of pounds in sick pay, loss of productivity and employees leaving for pastures new. Something has to be done about it.

The good news is that some organisations have taken the radical step of having 'no email' days, encouraging workers and suppliers to talk or meet with each other instead of relying on email. In some ways, this may seem like a backward step - but at least something is being done to better organise information sharing, particularly when it is of an iterative nature. Why not consider giving this a try yourself or putting it in place within your own business - you might be surprised at the results.

Training and education is mostly overlooked

One of the biggest issues that is frequently overlooked is that of providing any sort of training, education or guidance to employees on how to maintain a reasonable flow of information - and not to be part of the problem themselves. This is often because of the perceived benefit *versus* the cost of training; however, I doubt very much if the benefit analysis will have been rigorously undertaken because, if done, the value that could be derived from more effective information organisation and management would clearly outweigh, in the long-term, any employee training costs.

This is not an easy problem to address, of course. I like the story of the old farmer who was asked directions to a nearby village pub and, pondering and gesticulating, he replied, "Well, if wanted to get there, I wouldn't start from here, but you can go up there and turn left or go down there and turn right." We have a similar problem - we have to start somewhere...and training is as good a place as any.

Employees often need to be taught how to:

- Pick up the phone and make an appointment, or get to the salient points quickly, without then having to spend hours pinging back and forth dozens of time-wasting emails.

- Write an articulate email that contains all the relevant information in one email, rather than sending 10 or more individual emails, each containing what amounts to a clue or another part of the jigsaw puzzle. Each one has to be opened and assimilated and stored by the recipient.

- Clearly label the email in the subject box so that recipients know the basic content before they open it - this is also important to avoid the mail being sent straight to 'junk' by automated systems. The receiver will then be able to find the mail easily, because the subject title was completely meaningful and relevant. This type of labelling is known as *metadata* and is the 'information defining data in an information system'; the lack of it - and indeed sometime the complete absence of it - is frequently the cause of not being able to find information efficiently.

- Learn to pause before hitting the 'send' button - to ensure that the email is going to the correct recipient and, especially, check that you do not accidentally select 'reply to all', unless this is what you really want to do. Many an employee has been highly embarrassed by making a mistake here; some have even lost their jobs through inappropriate use of email.

- Check there are no glaring spelling or grammar mistakes by turning on your mail system's auto spellcheck facility - and that there is not a long string of other emails at the bottom of the one you are sending. This is especially true if you are 'forwarding' an email, which may contain, buried in the earlier exchanges, something that is not for the eyes of the recipient.

- Sift the wheat from the chaff; separate out what will normally be a very small number of emails that are meaningful in the context of everyday business.

- Turn off the 'new message notification' (the 'pinger' sound). This will enable them to become creative, productive and learn the power and bliss of an uninterrupted period of work.

- Using software to store your emails to be opened another day is not a solution. It just postpones the inevitable - one day waking up and acknowledging that you have thousands of unopened emails in your inbox.

- Understand the importance of virus prevention software and the problems a virus can cause if left unchecked.

- Keep personal and business emails quite separate from each other. Only deal with personal mail outside of business hours or, possibly, during lunch breaks. You are then much less likely to send a personal email, intended for your friend John Smithson, to your boss, John Smith, in error!

By no means should this list be considered exhaustive; it is important to remember that all of us are individuals - good practice for one may not necessarily be most appropriate good practice for another. In a full-blown information society you, as the Information Overlord, need tremendous flexibility when delivering solutions to the masses.

Password protected

Corporations are becoming increasingly aware that half their intellectual property is being stored on their employee's computers, laptops, tablets, blackberries and other mobile devices. They are also becoming aware that not only potential *assets* exist, but also contingent *liabilities* may be lurking away too. It is absolutely imperative that all devices are password-protected - but it is equally important that, should the employee fall sick (or under the proverbial bus), or resign or, for any other reason be unavailable, that other authorised management are able to access that employee's email and other important data. This protocol needs to be set up in advance of something dire happening. A record should also be kept of the important information that has been 'saved' during each of these events.

Metadata is so important - but often overlooked and misunderstood

The practice of labelling every single piece of information, so that it can be easily found and referred to by anyone who needs it, is a vital part of information management. We'll look at a number of ways to manage information in an expedient manner so that it may be found, not just in the coming days but, crucially, in the months and years ahead.

The true hero of metadata

Ted Nelson, the original pioneer of information technology, coined the phrases 'hypertext' and 'hypermedia' way back in the sixties and his dream with his *Xanadu Project* (*http://www.xanadu.com/*) was that all information could be linked together using foolproof systems. It's a real shame that, like so many visionaries who are ahead of their time, he never got full credit for his accomplishments. Nelson has been quoted many times in his career, but my two favourites of all are these:

"HTML is precisely what we were trying to prevent - ever-breaking links, links going outward only, quotes you can't follow to their origins, no version management, no rights management..."

and

"A user interface should be so simple that a beginner in an emergency can understand it within ten seconds."

http://xanadu.com.au/ted/

Lack of awareness, laziness and unwillingness

Even Ted Nelson, in all his wisdom, never predicted the sheer volume of information and emails we'd be showered with, in such a short space of time - and how that is still growing exponentially. Of course, the biggest problem we face is the *human element*: that of individuals not entering the correct metadata in the email subject fields, or labelling their own files logically, so others may, intuitively, find the information well into the future. It's in this area where training needs to grow and develop - regardless of what actual method of logging and organising information is ultimately used. The ultimate goal should be to put in place robust systems that are well-conceived, understood and embraced by management and employees alike and, in the end, will be self-sustaining.

Your days are numbered - and counting

The times I have received business plans that have no page numbers is legion. These days I always make a point of explaining to the sender that the secretary accidentally dropped the plan and pages went everywhere and we spent an hour or more trying to put them back in the right order, but in the end it was easier to number up the master copy and reprint...just to be sure. By dragging out and exaggerating this disaster story, perhaps next time they will remember to number every page of every single document. In this way, you can easily cross-reference things, and refer back to each page, by number, without having to coax someone through a 100-page document in the hopes they end up on the same page as you.

Alphabet soup

Letters are often used for keeping information in order and often, as you produce various drafts, you can label them 1a>1b>1c / 4a>4b>4c and so forth, so that readers are always aware that they are reading the latest version of a specific document. So much time is wasted with people working on, or reading, the wrong document.

For individuals and businesses, as well as the tools included in the latest incarnations of Microsoft Office (for example), there are now many online and offline automated 'version control systems' (VCS). Many content management systems (CMS) - the key infrastructure behind most of today's websites - provide excellent examples of version control systems in action.

These solutions can take away the pain of having to remember to manually mark up the latest iteration of a book or important report, therefore safeguarding key stakeholder inputs. Where they can add real value to the information management process, is as part of a large publication or website build project. I would recommend investing in one if you are thinking of developing any form of shared documentation or publication on which a number of people need to collaborate.

Pandora's Box

Once you start to manage information effectively, you tend to open up Pandora's Box - but the truth is you have to start somewhere. If you don't, death by information avalanche will swiftly beset you. There is no more painful death, not even death by chocolate. Once you are on top of *managing* emailing and simple filing, you then need to look at *organising* what, in your business, is likely to be your most valuable collateral and intellectual property:

- Assets management
- Debt management
- Procurement and contract management
- Project ledger

- Payroll and human resources
- Budget preparation and planning
- Marketing and research planning

Agendas in business meetings

To make the most of any meeting where information is shared, exchanged and, hopefully, acted upon, an agenda, preferably pre-circulated, is critical. The agenda should take the team through the meeting in a logical sequence; all topics should be covered in a meaningful way, in the right order and without having to go back to previous topics. A board meeting agenda should always begin with signing off the previous meeting's minutes, with everyone's agreement having had the prior weeks to lodge any queries. The agenda should always end with 'Any Other Business' (AOB), to ensure no one has further items they wish to table.

Background information papers

The background papers to cover every item on the agenda should be prepared well in advance of the meeting, so everyone has time to read the information and do their own research if necessary. It is unrealistic to expect attendees to read *and assimilate* information during the meeting. If they are reading, they aren't listening!

Sufficient background information, by way of bar charts, due diligence, contracts, quotes, research, company searches and any other material that is deemed necessary should be made available.

The person organising meetings should be aware of all this - and be aware that, by ignoring these basic rules, he or she is likely to get a bad press during or after the meeting.

Minutes

Accurate minutes of any formal meeting are crucial; these need to relate both negative and positive aspects of what was said, by whom and what was eventually agreed in the meeting. The dictionary definition of 'minutes' is 'formal and detailed record of business' (*http://www.businessdictionary.com*). This information remains in, and is, the history of the company; it may very well be relied upon many years later in internal disputes and sometimes in external court cases. Minutes are circulated to each member of the board by the secretary well in advance of the next meeting, to ensure that everyone is in agreement with what has been minuted. This gives sufficient time to make changes and challenges before they are signed off at the beginning of the next meeting. The minutes must then be stored safely and securely for future access.

Publishers and bookstores need to organise

Bookstores, publishers - and indeed the whole traditional publishing industry - now has to organise information more effectively because self-publishing and print-on-demand (POD) has changed the face of publishing as we know it. Organisation is called for, because of all the 'published' material out there - some is good, much is rubbish.

Publishers and bookstores try hard to deliver only qualified material that has gone through a stringent selection, verification and editing process. At the other end of the continuum, you can get your own book printed and published with a perfectly bound and beautifully illustrated cover for under a fiver - one copy at a time if you desire, or more if you have a marketplace for them. The content could be anything from brilliant literary genius to illiterate garbage. Poor quality self-publishers, who use Internet bookstores to distribute their product, eventually get caught out when their books get one-star reader rating scores on the likes of Amazon.com - or no sales!

Web designers: three seconds of fame, if you're lucky

Many website designers, and those commissioning websites, are still not aware how quickly the brain and eye works when it comes to scanning the computer screen for information. Even if their site appears on the first page of a search engine, such as Google, if the site description does not have the relevant metadata providing the viewer with *exactly* what they are looking for, the link will not be clicked on.

And then, even if it is clicked on, you only have around three to seven seconds to convince the person that they are on the right site and that you have the information they require. I personally do not stick around even that long. I can usually get the gist of site in under a second, and if it's not for me, I'm away. Website designers need to study the metrics of the sites they have built; designers, and the person marketing or owning the site, should put themselves in the viewer's shoes; they need to think through the information that is being offered, and consider how to alert the viewer immediately (and almost subconsciously) that the information they need is available somewhere on the site.

You need to be your own severest critic during this process and play around with site maps, colours, graphics and maybe images of *exactly* what you are offering. Let the visitor know what your site is about quickly, efficiently and intuitively.

I have spoken to many website designers about this and you can see them glazing over; you know they'll go back to their old ways and still be wondering why their sites are not 'sticky' and not performing. Only a small minority of Web people have got this bit right; they need to be thinking in terms of 'give the customer what information he needs' first and 'my interpretation of what the site should look like' second.

And I'm not the only one...

Trust me when I tell you I'm not the only one to work this particular magic. I combine modern technology with old-fashioned paper folders, box files and filing cabinets. Once I have taken on board a new client, I then take painstaking systematic care to save every single bit of email correspondence between that client and myself, so that I have a permanent record of everything that has been said and done. You cannot believe the times this has saved my bacon, allowed me to pull a rabbit of the hat and get ahead of the game.

The Information Overlord will have the expertise to integrate the old best practice ways of information management and organisation with today's modern, fast-paced technology driven information delivery systems.

ZOOM SECRETS

Your Personal Action Plan (8)

1. Only five to seven per cent of information is used effectively

The global value of information now to runs to $4.7 trillion annually and yet it is estimated that only five to seven per cent of information is used effectively. Among all corporate assets, information is the least understood and most poorly managed.

1. *What structures have you got in place to manage purchasing and storing of valuable information products and services?*

2. *Do an exercise to test if these structures serve their purpose.*

3. *Regularly audit your information assets and review usage/value with key stakeholders around your business.*

4. *Delete or archive information that is not being used or delivering value (now or in the future).*

2. Training and education is mostly overlooked

One of the biggest issues frequently overlooked is that of providing training to employees on how to maintain and effectively manage a reasonable flow of information. This is usually down to cost vs. perceived benefit of the training required.

1. *Do not make a training investment decision based on just gut feeling - carry out a rigorous benefit analysis that digs deep into the value that could be obtained from the information you have if it were properly managed and made available to the right people, at the right time and in the right format.*

2. *Pick a training partner that has a proven track record of developing skills in the area of your business that you are focusing on.*

3. *Select people to attend the training programme that will both manage **and champion** the use of information throughout your business or organisation.*

3. **Metadata is a powerful information management tool if properly understood and used**

> *The practice of labelling every single piece of information, so that it can be easily found and referred to by anyone who needs it, is a vital part of information management. Unfortunately, unless guided correctly, every individual will name/allocate metadata to information based on personal preference or style...*
>
> 1. Establish a business process whereby all employees use the same information naming conventions.
>
> 2. Ensure all new employees are inducted into this process the minute they join your business.
>
> 3. Take full advantage of version tracking functionality, often already built in the software you are using, including the MS Office suite of products.

4. **Once you start to manage information effectively, you can open up Pandora's Box...**

Once you are on top of managing emailing and simple filing, you then need to move on to organising your most valuable collateral and intellectual property.

1. *Identify the areas/processes of your business where the most valuable information resides - could it be Assets or Debt management? Procurement and contract management? Payroll and human resources? Marketing and research planning?*

2. *Consider giving responsibility for information management process monitoring and development of best practices to designated employees at a local department/function level, across the business.*

5. Managing information effectively and professionally during meetings is critical to business success

Meetings take up valuable business time and can be a complete diversion or waste of resources if not treated in a professional manner. To make the most of any meeting where information is shared and, hopefully, acted upon, an agenda should be created and pre-circulated to all attendees, together with any background information papers that need to be read before the meeting. Always keep a record (minutes) of what was agreed during the meeting and relevant action points - in many cases for board and trustee meetings, this can be a legal requirement.

1. *At your next business meeting, review structure, agenda and record keeping - are they all up to the standard required to properly manage the information flow?*

2. *Allocate on a rotating basis, agenda issue and minute taking if you are managing a team of people.*

3. *Ensure that all information produced is properly stored and backed up and that attendees know where to find that information in the future.*

CHAPTER 9

ONLINE INFORMATION AND REPUTATION MANAGEMENT

"Manage your reputation and become famous, not infamous"

Ron G Holland

I am convinced that 'Online Reputation Management' (ORM) is going to be the next big thing - but my research shows that most people currently involved in this burgeoning industry haven't yet got the bull by the horns. All too many of them are diving in at the deep end first, talking about the removal of negative information and publicity from the Internet - without really trying to discover or address the core problem. The Information Overlord will have thought this growing business issue through properly, developing an ORM strategy built not just on a reaction to negative information, but one that is fully integrated into a wider online marketing strategy and business best practice.

The core problem, of course, is that much of the negative publicity that needs to be removed or 'buried' (as most of the reputation management firms would have us believe) is actually caused by ourselves, our own incompetence and business mismanagement. A bitter pill to swallow perhaps - but nevertheless true.

The other aspect of reputation management is that it is so big, yet so subtle. It really is an all-encompassing web that is so close to us, we often can't see the wood for the trees. Let's look at a few things that will massively enhance our online information presence and improve our reputations before we delve into how things may or may not be removed or 'buried'.

Now is the time to start building and maintaining a good reputation online. Here are a few tips that may surprise you:

It's more about taking *preventative* measures, than *remedial* actions

People generally - and employees in particular - need to understand and remember that once information has been emailed or published to a website, such as Facebook or Twitter for example, it is very hard to remove. Preventative measures include developing best business practices throughout each stage, and every level, of your organisation.

It is time to do your own thinking and start developing strategies and methodologies based on common sense. You'll stop making a rod for your own back - and stop incurring contingent liabilities, that will have to be cleared away in the future. *Now* is the time to develop a code of ethics that will serve you, your employees and your customers well, keep your online reputation intact - and keep you out of trouble.

Spelling and Grammar

They often say that charity begins at home but I sincerely believe that, when it comes to online information and online reputations, we must start looking at ourselves and our employees and start to create just the right reputation needed for long-term, sustained success. Many times I see business owners being their own worst enemies. Let me give you a few examples.

I know the consensus of opinion says that spelling and grammar doesn't matter that much on the Internet. But the truth is it does, much more than you could possibly realise - particularly when you are in business.

This is not a book on grammar, but getting to grips with simple words like 'their' and 'there' - or 'your' and 'you're' - is crucial to anyone writing even the most simple business letter. I see, practically every single day, something on the lines of:

I trust <u>your</u> OK and I'll see you over <u>their</u> at 8pm.

Only last week I saw someone referring to their *sauce* when they really meant *source*. It's only a small thing, but not when you're telling people you can manage their reputations!

It is totally unacceptable to be asking for business, putting in quotes and offering advice when your information is riddled with typos, missing words and bad grammar.

Your LinkedIn and social media profiles

This is another example where most business people do not pay anything like enough care and attention to ensure their profiles are the best they can be. Maybe times there are gaps in their information and, worse still, misleading information. This is not good enough, especially when you consider that many executives will automatically check out your profile if they come across your name, or are recommended to you by someone else. It's second nature these days to do your own form of 'due diligence' on people you may be doing business with, so you need to ensure your profile is as sharp and as accurate as it can possibly be. Obviously, this takes a serious amount of executive time and effort, but you will certainly reap the rewards in the future.

Refund policies that work

My first book, *Debt Free with Financial Kung Fu* came out 1977, over 30 years ago. We sold thousands of copies, selling it mail order using full-page adverts in magazines like *Exchange & Mart*. It wasn't long before the Office of Fair Trading, or whatever it was called at the time, was knocking at my door telling me about a complaint. I told him that was absolutely impossible; we had mechanisms in place that made it so. The guy was insistent, so I invited him in for tea and he showed me the letter of complaint where the customer was complaining that he never received a refund. I quickly went to my files and dug out the guy's UNCASHED cheque and gave it to the official. His mouth dropped open. It didn't take too much explaining to show that there was a 30-day money back guarantee on the book and we never even bothered to cash anyone's cheque for at least *sixty* days. The official commented that I was an outstanding businessman, could see I was running a completely legitimate business and off he waddled down the road clutching the uncashed cheque in his hand, after stuffing himself with tea and all my chocolate biscuits. Two weeks later, I got another cheque from the same customer for TWO books explaining what a brilliant book it was after all and how he had made a big mistake.

What is called for today, both offline and online, are much more robust refund policies that keep your customers happy - and you out of trouble with Trading Standards authorities or the various television or radio 'customer champions'. Nowadays, it is even more important that you develop customer-focused policies; if you don't, those customers will soon be voicing their concern on the many forums out there on the Internet, including the eCommerce website where they quite likely bought the product in the first place. A poor customer experience can very quickly lead to a poor online reputation and, in the worse case, your eCommerce site closing down.

Refund policies that don't work

I don't need to mention names, because you can do your own research and find dozens of people who have sold high-price workshops, seminars and Internet marketing and money-making products for thousands.

Unfortunately for the consumer, many unscrupulous promoters not only didn't have a refund policy in place, but absolutely refused to return anyone's money - and then wondered why they were deluged with hundreds, or even thousands, of negative reviews and complaints. I have heard from a reliable source that many of them now spend more money with reputation managers, trying hard to bury all these negative comments, than it would have cost them to settle the refunds.

Over-exaggerated claims

The Information Overlord will be careful in everything that he or she does to create the most powerful, creditable impression - without over-egging the pudding. All too often, amateurs make false claims that usually come back to haunt them. Recently in California, for the first time in US history, new legislation allows a firm to be fined up to $11,000 for every false claim that they make. Taking the diligence one step further, you need to ensure that employees and affiliate marketers don't get carried away with their enthusiasm, and try to make extra sales by making false or misleading claims. At the end of the day, it will be *your* reputation brought into doubt.

Disclaimers and Terms & Conditions

Over the past few years, you may have noticed a proliferation of disclaimers being placed at the bottom of emails. This is because more and more businesspeople have become aware of legal threats and have, thus, started managing their reputations and online information.

Disclaimers can offer protection in all sorts of cases, including breach of confidentiality, transmission of viruses, entering into contracts, negligent statements and employee's liability. Many times these disclaimers are even added to internal email - and there have been numerous cases where employees have been disciplined, or even dismissed, for sending emails with racist, sexual and other offensive content. And remember - the 'joke' email sent to just one or two people internally, can so easily be forwarded to people outside.

Every eCommerce website nowadays must have terms and conditions attached; you have probably noticed that, every time you send off for something or join a new service, you need to check the box that says you have read the terms and conditions. Maybe you don't want to - but you will not get any further until you do. If you do care to read the terms and conditions, you will observe that companies are getting more and more vigilant and pedantic in the terms that they are getting you to agree to, all as part of the online information procedures and reputation management processes that website owners are now employing.

Don't Mislead Customers

Misleading customers is guaranteed to get you into trouble. Customers hate to be misled, so let them know exactly what they will be getting into. For example, a lot of Internet marketers and newbies to business make the mistake of misleading customers by making outrageous claims about their products or services. They think they are writing good copy but, in the process, can mislead customers into thinking or perceiving things which are simply not true. Get your copy checked and edited. In situations where genuine mistakes have been made, and your customers pick up on this, do whatever it takes to resolve the issues with those customers to maintain your integrity. The last thing you want is an unhappy customer blogging to their social following of hundreds or thousands, causing you more harm than good.

Setting social media policies in the workplace

Currently, only a minority of companies have internal social media policies, but that trend is changing. What has become apparent is the ones that do have such policies in place are agreeing on one thing - that they assist in keeping up productivity. As well as creating clear guidelines as to when employees can access Twitter, Wikipedia, MySpace, Facebook or Yelp, make it clear to employees that, if they contribute to any of these, exactly what kind of information they can impart. They need to protect the company's confidential information and never comment on anything legal. If they must write about the competition, make sure it is in friendly and diplomatic terms. They should only post meaningful and respectful comments and steer clear of spam - and never refer to the company in a dishonest or misleading way.

Subscribe to Google alerts

You need to regularly monitor what is being said about you, your company or your brand online. Subscribing to 'Google Alerts' to get up-to-date entries about your name and brand every day is a must - and very easy to set up. Don't wait for a dip in your business to occur; find out who is saying what, right now. It is also very easy, at the same time, to set up a separate alert to monitor your competitor's coverage as well - be one step ahead!

Negative postings or information could ruin your reputation and business online. The Internet contains thousands of different ways for consumers and businesses to interact with you as well as each other. Social media, videos, articles, blogs, social profiles, press releases, social bookmarks, mobile sites, phone apps - these are just some of the things you must have in place to allow you to be found in today's highly fragmented online marketplace. However, these same media could also spell disaster for you if not monitored professionally and regularly. If Google Alerts does inform you of anything negative, you should act on it immediately.

BUILD YOUR REPUTATION

In today's digital world, your information is more widely available - and to more people than ever before. Building an online presence is now a major part of the marketing mix for any new business venture. Visibility will get you more traffic, which should translate into more customers, more sales. With the emergence of social media, mobile and new technology, maintaining brand reputation is becoming equally as important. However, you need to build visibility and a strong online presence first. Just remember though, you have a clean sheet of paper when setting up online for the first time. *This is the only opportunity you will ever get to put in place the foundations needed to create a positive and enviable online reputation.*

To make sure you get it right the first time, carry out some research with family, friends and your target audience - before you launch. Learn from the feedback you get, make the changes needed and then you will be in a position to launch with the best possible scenario for building a strong, positive reputation online.

On the one hand…. "You don't have a presence on the Web."

I remember the day well when a potential client came up to me and said, "You don't have a presence on the Web. I can't find you anywhere."

I was mortified, especially after having paid various website designers and other promoters to put up sites, drive traffic, make videos and deliver all the tools and services. It was particularly galling, because I had invested quite large amounts of money with some of them. Like all Information Overlords, I decided to get into action and get meaningful information into the right places. Lots of it!

On the other ... "I can't believe what I'm seeing, you're everywhere."

The action was mind-power work; I decided to attract to me a webmaster who could not only build websites, but drive traffic, handle social media, blogging, videos, and just about everything else. The one thing I learned from my new webmaster, Jatinder, was that because the Internet is so vast you have to be extremely diligent in what you do - and do a lot of everything and keep on doing it and never stop. We really did create hundreds of articles, blogs, videos and pictures. We developed a serious presence on social media sites and undertook huge amounts of search engine optimisation (SEO) work. All just for starters. Now here's another clue. Those articles took a lot of time, thought and research to get just the right information - and then serious quality writing time, often between the hours of 5am and 7am. We now get lots of positive comments and have many followers, for the niche that we operate in.

Unfortunately, as many people are in such a rush these days, they don't seem to have the patience or necessary skills to carry out a similar exercise. They are often their own worst enemies, writing gobbledegook rubbish that has no meaningful content and is neither aspirational nor inspirational. They are, in effect, damaging their own online reputations, often without even realising it.

To build a reputation you have to do everything - and do it correctly

Building a positive reputation online takes hard work, but as the Information Overlord knows, is well worth the effort. When it comes to the use of the Internet, things are changing fast; don't think that, because something has worked for you in the past, it will work for you in the future. As a business owner, you have to keep changing; go with the flow, if you want to stand out and stomp on your competition. The Internet has become the main tool that many consumers now turn to before purchasing even local products and services. While this may seem like a great opportunity to expose your business to local consumers, it can also have a negative impact if proper reputation management procedures are not put in place. Unfortunately, many businesses are plagued by false information and slander and don't even realise it, resulting in lost sales before a potential customer has even entered their website. But if you don't know about it, how can you fix it?

You are who Google says you are

You need to find a way of dominating the front page of Google with your name, business and chosen subject. The way to do this, of course, is to 'do it all and do lots of it!' We had great fun getting one of my sites, *wealth.co.uk* from about page 50 to the front page of Google. I wrote hundreds of articles, and got huge amounts of good quality information into the right places. Jatinder put up videos and started blogging and creating backlinks. It took us a couple of months, but we did it and it was well worthwhile, as I know I now have one of the most easily found - and positive - profiles on the Internet.

Blog frequently

This can help your customers stay up to date with your business. Blogs give plenty of information for people to find out more about you. It keeps them informed and allows you to share and connect with your existing and new customers. When you come across useful information, don't you share this with your peers? If you do this, it then allows others to share too; by providing only quality information, it helps maintain all participating parties' online reputation. Build that reputation and rapport by being perceived as an expert authority in your field. This only happens when you walk the walk and not just talk the talk.

Create videos that inform

Creating a targeted video for your audience is a powerful tool, if you can deliver just the right level of information they are looking for. Take care to think about the backdrop in the recording - and make sure you script each video so the commentary flows. Deliver 'bite-sized' chunks of punchy information, leaving the viewer with their tongue hanging out for more. People's attention span is very limited, so about three to four minutes should do the trick. Creating links and a 'call to action' is the secret. Just remember though, video is fast becoming the information source of choice for many people and is therefore the medium that will probably have the most impact on your online reputation.

Shoot photos that inspire

A frequently overlooked, but ever-increasing, search trend is 'images'; if you can dominate all the images under your name, niche and brand, so much the better. Get creative and use different locations, products, bright images, designer clothes, colours and backdrops. Make sure each image has meta tags leading the viewer to where you want them to go for further information. Good quality photos of you, your company and products can create a really positive online image - poor photos can, of course, create just the opposite effect.

Use social networks

Connecting with people and maintaining pages on the popular social media sites such as Facebook will also enhance search engine results. Interacting with your customer base allows you to monitor what people say, like and dislike. Social activity can cause a viral effect and allow you to reach out to more people than you could ever imagine. Engaging in social media in a proactive way is one of the quickest ways to create a loyal following and build a solid online reputation, but it does require a regular focus as 'new news' rapidly becomes 'old news'.

Offer useful online content

Providing useful, valuable content, particularly in a niche market, is an extremely powerful way of building your online brand and reputation. Add value to your customers' experiences, so it can cast *your* business in a positive light; aim to be the expert authority in your field. Having a well-researched resource area of free downloads or bonuses for your customers will encourage them to come back - and will also add to building your trust and reputation. Importantly, it will also encourage your loyal followers to share the word about your useful content with others, leading to increasing levels of website visits. This is how viral marketing starts off.

Highlight customer testimonials

With permission, of course and without any laws. If you can get 'trusted' video testimonials, they will have the most impact. Viewers can see the other people and relate to the subject matter better. Testimonials can also counter any complaints, because it shows the results you can, or have, achieved, for your clients or customers. As you build your reputation, your database of preferred customers will grow. These people will buy from you over and over again; every now and then it is quite acceptable to ask them for written and video testimonials.

Ensure that all information on your website is accurate

Do not treat your website like a personal web page; keep all content professional and business-related. Your landing page - your homepage - is most likely the beginning of your reputation journey. Remember the old adage - you never get a second chance to make a first impression!

Make sure the information on the front page is accurate and well written. Ensure all the links work; provide a map of where you are - and check that your postcode is accurate and allows the use of satellite navigations systems or online mapping. You know exactly where your office or workshop is, but your customers don't! Make sure your terms and conditions have been checked by your legal advisers. This will be the first thing that merchant account providers check before they agree to let you have credit card processing facilities.

Be courteous in your public posts and responses; never argue with a customer or reply with rude comments. Your goal is to win over customers, not to make enemies, so keep correspondence professional at all times and maintain your composure - even (especially) when it seems impossible. It will pay off in the long run. Lose your cool, and you could set yourself and business up to miss out on massive new business and potential growth.

REPAIR YOUR REPUTATION

If you do find yourself in a situation whereby you need to repair your reputation, it will pay dividends to get to the bottom of exactly who or what it is that is causing you grief. Only then will you know how to respond in the most precise manner to bring about the best possible results. The best plan of action is to separate out, into two lists, criticisms that may very well be deserved, and those that are not. To come to a quick conclusion that you may want to bury any negative information is just naive; it's time to do some serious analysis to see why people are negative towards you and your company. These days, no one is exempt; even lawyers, accountants, dentists, doctors and other professionals can find business dipping off because of negative comments people have made.

Deserved attacks may, possibly, include requests for refunds that you have not responded to quickly enough; that you have not abided by your terms and conditions; ambiguities, product failures, service not up to standard or some other reason why a genuine customer has felt aggrieved.

Undeserved attacks may include vicious attacks from disgruntled former employees or unscrupulous competitors; people who are libellous, out-and-out liars, or others defaming your character; a jealous ex-partner, mistaken identity - or some other reason why someone, either by name or anonymously, has commented negatively.

Deserved attacks

No one really deserves to be attacked. Here I mean genuine customers who paid for goods and services, but now, for one reason or another, feel aggrieved. By far the best way is to communicate with them on a one-on-one basis; try, if at all possible, to come to a compromise. Get to the bottom of what is happening and then come to some sort of agreement that makes everyone happy. Whatever that agreement is, it should include the customer removing any negative comments as part of the package. Sometimes it is well worth investing in a 'customer service' department to ensure that every single complaint is dealt with in a careful and professional manner. In the end, the goodwill created by this commitment will bring not only repeat business but, most likely, referrals as well.

Set up a 'customer service centre' to become a profit, not a cost centre

I remember reading a story about James Dyson when he first set up selling Dyson vacuum cleaners. He had a number of complaints until he hired a full-time adviser to set up a service centre to sort it all out. The adviser, as I remember the story, made sure that all faulty vacuum cleaners were replaced within 24 hours and the faulty ones stripped down and put back into stock. The whole operation was so slick. Dyson must be doing something right; he made over £300 million profit in 2011 and has a positive online reputation to boot!

"It'll be there forever" is not necessarily true

In my experience, the people who claim that, "information put up on the web will be there forever" are really saying, "I just haven't got a clue about how to remove negative information." But when you think about it, all information is put up by a person somewhere, on a computer or server that is sited somewhere and all of it hosted by an Internet Service Provider (ISP). Not too much rocket science involved, nor too many steps required tracking back to guilty parties and bringing pressure to bear to get them to remove the offending information.

If you come across sites that have negative content about you, politely ask for the negative comments or review to be removed; there is nothing wrong with asking especially where content is clearly a direct attack.

On occasion, the ISP may be able to help you get the offending information removed, especially if it thinks it is going to be embroiled in some legal case. Sometimes you have to 'prove' your case and point of view to the ISP; it may very well get back to the offending party and ask for their point of view. In my experience, however, the offending party does not usually even reply to the ISP and then the ISP will quickly remove the offending information where it is within its control.

If this tactic doesn't work, you may have to go to the expense of hiring a lawyer or specialist reputation management consultant, but do choose one with substantial experience in this area.

Use the power of positive SEO to detract from negative information

Swamp the negative. For argument's sake, let's assume someone says you are operating a 'scam'. You may want to consider writing hundreds of articles about scams and making an equal number of videos, and get these posted all over the Internet - using, for example, PRWeb or TubeMogul.

In this way, people searching for your name or company's name are more likely to come across your own articles and videos before any negative information, thereby creating the right impression.

Respond to Valid Criticism and Claims

This shows you care! Interact with your customers and seek their opinions so that you can improve your communication and service processes. This shows that you do listen to your customers. We all have our faults and vulnerabilities. People do understand, but show that you action this too.

Be Transparent

If something goes wrong, let your customers know - and let them know how you are addressing the situation. We all like to be kept in the loop, so we are not left in the dark to wonder. The mind will try to fill the gaps and could put anything in there, so ensure your customers are not under any illusions. Keep them in the loop by letting them know exactly what is going on. Remember to follow up; don't say you will do something and then not do it. If you are getting lots of complaints, or people begin to talk about you, then you need to look at your business and customer service processes.

You need to get on top of the situation and fix it right away. You may need to get outside help, but just do it. Do what it takes to maintain honesty and integrity in your business. As the Information Overlord knows, the consequences of not remaining transparent when things go wrong can be dire, particularly if the national media become involved.

Create a Customer Forum

If a customer complains, is it not better that they complain on your own forum rather than outside? This way you can address the situation without drawing too much attention.

A forum for your customers may end up helping thousands understand how something works. It is possible that people buy things and are unsure how to use them, or they have compatibility issues. If these things are present on forums, it becomes another support area for your customers - as well as providing your technical and product research teams with valuable usability feedback. You can also interact within the forum to help your customers, again building that positive reputation. Treat all your online customers with the utmost of respect. Always reply to responses made by them - never ignore a customer. Try to remain as engaging with your audience as you can, on a professional level.

Never leave your reputation to chance

As difficult as it may seem sometimes, you should never let your reputation be left to chance. Having a good reputation is crucial to the growth of your business, therefore it's critical that you focus on building a strong, positive online reputation that will make doing business with you a 'no-brainer' for your target market.

Remember the Internet is the gateway to the world; if you use it wisely, you will reap its rewards. If you are not able to maintain a good online reputation, your business is likely to feel the brunt of those consequences, which could ultimately cost you thousands. You not only want to get letter writing, engaging lawyers and creating articles and videos that will counter all negative comment under your belt, but you'll also want to consider the other things we have discussed in this chapter which, if applied holistically, will help create a positive reputation that will counter and indeed help 'bury' any bad information you may have out there.

Commissioning a specialist Online Reputation Management Consultant

When your business has got to such a size and stature that managing your online reputation in-house becomes a significant drain on resources, as well as a potential distraction, it might be time to bring in an expert - either to help clean up your existing information trail or to manage things on an ongoing basis.

There are lots of people out there claiming to be experts. Ideally you should aim to find a partner with a proven track record and, above all, someone who is trustworthy and is able to understand the commercial reality of your business. A web design agency with strong search engine optimisation (SEO) skills would be a good place to start, as this will underpin all the online reputation building 'technical' work that would have to take place. Do not, however, expect this to be an overnight exercise. Typically ORM projects can take a number of weeks - or even months - depending on the amount of work required.

Things to consider before commissioning an ORM Consultant:

- Must be digital savvy and have excellent SEO skills
- Must have an analytical mind
- Must have a proven Web presence of their own
- Must be highly literate
- Must have the right tools to track performance
- Must have a proven track record in ORM

ZOOM SECRETS

Your Personal Action Plan (9)

Reputation management is more about taking preventative measures, than remedial actions

Once information has been emailed or published to a website, it is very hard to remove. Individuals and businesses must put in place preventative measures and sound strategies based on common sense. Now is the time to develop a code of ethics that will serve you, your employees and your customers well and help to keep your reputation intact.

Remember:

1. *Spelling and grammar really counts - always use a spellchecker before publishing or emailing.*

2. *Customers come first - make sure your refund policy really works so that it creates positive feedback.*

3. *Regularly communicate positive news with customers via blogs/social media.*

4. To shout about your achievements and great offers but make sure you are not stretching the truth as it might haunt you for a long time - note down the potential top five:

-
-
-
-
-

5. To have policies about using social media by your employees - help them build your reputation, not hinder it.

6. To make sure that people can easily find you on the Web.

7. To capitalise on your customer testimonials - make sure they are visible everywhere, but not in a blatant fashion.

8. To turn all attacks on you into a victory - show how caring you are and how you solve all the issues - but you must be able to deliver on this promise.

9. If all else fails, consider hiring reputation management experts - it might be a very wise investment for the future.

CHAPTER 10

A MIND OF INFORMATION

"Only when we have learned how to 'not think' as well as 'think' will our minds work like they are supposed to, like problem-solving computers."

Ron G Holland

Without doubt, our heads are full of information. I have spent the last 30 years studying why some people succeed and indeed excel - while others, even though their heads may also be crammed with information, never even get past the starting point. Let's examine a few concepts, based on my personal experience as well as my research, that will give you the winner's edge.

The Brain's Information Superhighway

The vast majority of people are just not aware of their thought processes. For you to become an Information Overlord, it is crucial you become aware of what is going on in your brain. A simple model of the brain shows that it consists of two separate hemispheres, the right and left-brain; they process information in two totally different ways. The left brain processes in words: it is analytical, logical and sequential. The right brain processes in images: it is highly creative and is the domain of artists, dreamers, visionaries and successful entrepreneurs. The two hemispheres are joined together with a substantial band of nerve fibres, the corpus callosum, which is the brain's 'information highway'. It allows the words in the left brain to communicate with the images in the right brain.

The filter of the brain is called the reticular activating system (RAS) and is at the top of the brain stem; it checks and monitors the flow of information into the two halves of the brain. This is the mechanism the hypnotherapist deactivates, in order to plant ideas and suggestions way below the threshold of consciousness.

Many folk in the west are predominantly left-brained, thinking mostly in words, as a result of an education system that stopped them thinking in pictures. However, this trend has started to reverse with the advent of the Internet. So much information is now being conveyed in images - on the TV, videos, graphs, cartoons and picture books. Most kids these days hate to read a long book full of text and no pictures. Pictures bring words to life, of course and, when used together, provide a powerful learning and production tool that no man-made computer can - as yet - beat.

Start using your in-built Broadband - you'll notice the difference

Many folk who seem to be continually tired are trying to run their lives by processing huge amounts of information - and trying to solve problems on their left brains alone. They wonder why they don't get anywhere. Those who have their act together have learned how to think in images *and* words and get the information flowing between the two sides of their brains, via the corpus callosum - your own personal broadband. This is called 'whole-brain thinking' and it is an essential tool of the Information Overlord. People who think in pictures as much as they do in words are highly creative, problem solvers, happy, masters of information *and* their own destinies.

Meditation

I have deliberately put meditation at the head of the list because I firmly believe that everyone, not only stressed executives, will benefit substantially if they take on board this practice. It was in 1981 when *Talk & Grow Rich* first came out, when I was living in the States. The first chapter of the book was entitled *The Principle of Power* and it woke up a lot of people. This was the first time a book on selling and making money had majored on meditation. My formula, *Silence, Stillness and Solitude ($$$)* attracted a lot of attention and many self-help authors now include meditation as part of their routine.

The secret of meditation is to go out of your mind and not think of anything, starting with as little as five or ten minutes a day. The Japanese call this practice 'Satori' which is 'no mind'. Of course, none of this is easy - but it is worth the effort; even if you just 'go through the motions', you will eventually get there and attain demonstrable results in the way of ideas, hunches, guidance and even Eurekas from your subconscious mind. In the east, they say, 'By going out of our minds once a day, we come to our senses'.

When in the state of meditation we slip into Alpha, and in that state our brains, the right and left hemispheres, sift and sort all the information we have in our minds and make sense of it. It is paradoxical, that the less we think, the more powerful our thoughts become; in meditation the idea is to try to stop the thoughts completely. Stop the internal dialogue and you can hear the Eurekas!

Goal setting

In the east, where meditation originated, many benefits were discovered by slipping into 'no mind' on a regular basis. These included tranquillity, bliss, spirituality, enlightenment and peace of mind. In the materialistic west, we need to add another dimension in order to gain the most from our minds, to suit the culture that we live in. To get meditation working optimally, we must link it to *goal setting* so that we may solve problems, attain goals and be competitive. We not only need to set goals in our personal lives for the things we want to attain for ourselves, but also in our business lives and careers. It pays to write them down; the more detailed those goals are, the better. Add as many practical ways - as well as *impractical* ways - of attaining them. The mind works like a computer and needs input information to compute its answers, so the more 'input information' - and the better the quality of that information - you can provide, will help it along. The biocomputer, as I prefer to call the mind, will fill in all the missing gaps and give you startling ideas, hunches and Eurekas to help you attain your goals.

Visualisation of information

There is quite a bit involved in reprogramming your mind to get the best possible output.

Let's assume you have accepted the discipline, for that is all it is, of meditating every day (preferably twice a day) and going into 'no mind', the ultimate state for creativity and problem solving. Let's also assume you have set some personal goals for your life and business and now want to upload all of that information into your biocomputer in the most expedient manner. The starting point is to read your goals aloud (onto an audio-cassette or MP3 player or smartphone, if at all possible); then immediately visualise that goal in your mind's eye. In that way you program, in words and pictures simultaneously, to both your left and right brain.

The whole idea is to *visualise* as much as you can of each goal in as great a detail as possible. If you don't know where the money is coming from for your new Porsche, visualise it anyway; see yourself driving it and having loads of fun in it - in great detail. If you don't know who is going to write the copy for your new marketing concept, visualise as much as you can of a successful advertising campaign anyway. The secret is to use your 'imagination' and 'see' things happening in your mind's eye - even when you know they can't or won't or shouldn't, simply because you don't have the resources to hand. Use your imagination to overcome all that and 'see' your goals happening. The more 'information input', in the way of words, images, sounds or smells, that you can add to your visualisations, the better. The bio-computer is great at connecting up all the dots and coming up with a foolproof plan for success - but it needs lots of 'information input' as grist for its subconscious mill.

The paradigm shift

This is something that I have created for myself on a regular basis and, more importantly, have been able to teach to others - who have gone on to create significant results, in some instances far greater than my own successes. When I was 20, I was just finishing my apprenticeship as a carpenter and joiner; my father had rightly insisted that I start and see this through to the very end. However, the day I finished the apprenticeship, I set up my first motorcycle shop! Everyone laughed, because I had begun a business in an industry that I had not been trained for - and only had one motorcycle for sale in the shop.

What most people didn't know, and couldn't possibly know, was that I had trained my brain for a massive paradigm shift going from *carpentry* to *motorcycles*. In the preceding months, I had flooded my neurons with positive images of me in my own shop, selling and repairing motorcycles. I did this many times, like running a film in my brain of the future that I was going to create for myself. I had obviously trained and reprogrammed my brain pretty well, because within a few short years I ended up with the largest chain of motorcycle shops in south London - and accidentally picked up two furniture shops and a forty-bedroom hotel on the way!

I got myself to the States

Using this same methodology, I began to visualise, over and over again, that I had sold the motorcycle shops at a good profit - and was now living in the States as a full-time business author. I even made trips to Heathrow Airport and visualised myself getting on a plane. Very quickly, I found myself living in Beverley Hills writing books and earning a living as a motivational speaker. Thirty years on, I have now helped many people create their own paradigm shifts; those who carried it off successfully always managed to dream, in carefully choreographed pictures in their mind's eyes, of what they would be doing in the future.

Aptitude

I have noted that many people are not cut out for IT, design, singing, selling or accountancy. Others seem to be able to turn their hands to brain surgery, haircutting, mentoring, teaching and carpentry. Aptitude has a lot to do with what you love doing and also what you get trained to do, the environment that you grew up in and, of course, all the valuable information you have gained on the way. I used to relish stories of wartime armed forces recruiting people, and get them to stand in line. The drill sergeant would bark, "You 50 are going to volunteer to become electricians, you lot carpenters, you lot airplane mechanics." And so it went on. There was no argument, yet many of those assigned found they did have a natural ability to learn and do the things they were required to do, once the correct training had been given to them. The point is that many of these people would never have chosen, of their own free will, to be a mechanic or a cook - they would have 'self-censored' the thoughts before they could be acted upon. But when it was thrust upon them, their natural ability could come to the fore.

One of my favourite expressions that I use at my workshops is, "Do something that you can do." So often, I find people who have invested relatively large sums of money to teach them how to make fortunes from Internet Marketing, Social Media or online trading - only to get home and realise the last thing that they really want to do is spend time at home staring at a reluctant uncooperative computer that won't deliver hits, sales or any other kind of meaningful result.

Attitude

It's trite but true; your attitude affects your altitude. Funnily enough, your attitude is one thing you can control, whatever your circumstance, if you care to do so. Enthusiasm is one of those things that is crucial to success in both your personal and business life, yet so many people seem to lack it. Of course, you can control this and I suggest that you do just that by 'acting enthusiastically'. Even if you're not enthusiastic, 'act as though you are' and soon genuine enthusiasm will take over. You'll notice those around you will want to be part of the show and they too, will start to get enthusiastic. This can be of particular importance if you are sharing face-to-face, with friends or work colleagues, large amounts of relatively boring information that you want people to really understand and take note of.

Get yourself a mentor

A mentor is going to be a mine of information, way ahead of where you're currently at; if you get a good one, they'll patiently hold your hand and guide you through a step-by-step process of taking you (or helping you get to) exactly where you want to go. I am minded of the expression, 'Hitch your wagon to a star' and I have always strived to rub shoulders with clever people: mathematicians, scientists, physicists, actors, millionaires and billionaires. The other expression I like, and have found true on many occasions is, 'When the student is ready, the master appears.' I have kept myself in state of readiness, always in a position to tag along with someone older, wiser, more astute - and earn and learn as I go along.

What I have discovered is that most of the people who have been there and done it, love to share the information and the secrets of their success with their apprentices.

The ideal mentor is *not* your line manager; maybe a senior executive elsewhere in the organisation - someone with whom you have no real reason to be involved with on a day-to-day basis. Maybe someone outside of your organisation, but the issue of confidentiality of information *may* influence some of your conversations. Choose a non-competing organisation. Many Business Link type organisations offer a mentoring service, so explore this with them.

Assimilating Information

Information Overlords, by definition, will be heavily involved in information; they'll know how to assimilate huge amounts of it, without stress or detriment. I learned a number of speed reading techniques that changed the course of my life and I will share these with you. Being able to assimilate massive amounts of information very quickly helps me enormously when I take on a new client, and want to get up to speed very quickly with the industry that he or she is in. The techniques I use are so effective that, many times, I can surpass my clients' views and understanding of the industry that they are in and be in a position to pass on leading ideas that may really give them a quantum leap. I also use the techniques when I am researching a new book and want to get huge amounts of information into my brain in the shortest space of time. Of course, there are many speed reading courses out there and I suggest you investigate them - but this is what I do.

It doesn't really matter whether it is a book, a client or something else I am researching and trying to get my mind around; the following works for me, and I have been using these techniques successfully for years.

The Internet truly is the definitive source of information for me. I start by Googling, with as many search terms as I can think of, the subject in hand. I save everything as I go, including stuff that may possibly have no use or relevance at all. At this stage I want to capture it all while it is showing itself. I already know that 98% of all the stuff I save and view will be no good to me, but what I want are clues leading me to the valuable nuggets. As the stuff appears on the screen, I scan the key headlines; I absolutely know that, if my eyes see the information, the brain acts like a scanner, and that information is going to end up somewhere inside my brain.

After a few days or, sometimes, a few weeks, depending how big the project is, I will have a huge quantity of saved web pages to get through; now I will sit myself down, armed with copious supplies of tea and coffee, and aim to wade through all this material. I don't *read* it, I *skim* through it - looking for headlines, subheadings, words and pictures that jump off the screen at me. I emphasise - I still do not spend too much time *reading*, I am skimming, looking for nuggets. All I want is nuggets and insights and I highlight these as I go.

The final step is to load up with more coffee and get comfortable for a proper read. By now, I have whittled down hundreds, maybe even thousands, of pages to just a few that I have highlighted; it is these I read with interest. Here's another big clue. Even though I know what I have to read, I still give all the highlighted materials just one more skim, to let my brain soak up as much of what is on the pages as possible. Only then will I go about a steady read, more highlighting and cutting out and saving the bits I really want.

This is the final clue. We now need to assimilate all that information *in our minds* using every part of our biocomputers. The real magic happens when we use words, pictures, our reticular activating system and the corpus callosum in the processing phase. I know the information is just information, until it has been through the biocomputer and merged with all the other information - and added the vital ingredients of imagination and creativity. This is called *assimilation.* When you do this, you create books, products, solutions for clients and much, much more. Most people never learn this extraordinary but simple skill and they remain ordinary.

When I do the final read, I carefully take on board the words, but I also turn those words into pictures and try hard to *visualise* what the story, article or picture is all about. At the end of the process, I visualise everything coming together, in one big collage.

In essence, I get my brain working like a biocomputer to compute for me something exemplary and seminal out of all the materials I have programmed into it. Once this is all done, the product I end up with is much greater than the sum of all the parts.

Applying these techniques day-to-day

The power and capability of the mind to manage vast amounts of information is absolutely amazing. How many computers are there still around and working after 70, 80 or 90 years of life, that can still retrieve memories that go back that many years? The human brain is the computer of the future - how many years will it take, if ever, to fully replicate it with technology? The good thing is that we can take advantage of that bio-technology now, simply by putting in place the techniques that I have outlined in this chapter and that the Information Overlord excels in.

You will no doubt be thinking, "But how will I find time to do these things - and where can I find the right place and space to carry them out?"

At home, take time out to think and practice when carrying out mundane tasks such as washing up, dusting, vacuuming the floor etc. Many of my Eureka! moments often happen when I am in the bath - also another great place to practice meditation and visualise and, apocryphally, the birthplace of the original Eureka moment! In the office, take time out during a lunch break in a quiet place or vacant office. You might even find, through discussion of this topic, other like-minded colleagues who would be open to setting up a 'mind of information' group that could meet on a weekly basis, in or outside of the office.

ZOOM SECRETS

Your Personal Action Plan (10)

1. Start using your in-built Broadband - you'll notice the difference

> *Those who have got their act together have learned how to think in images and words and get the information flowing between the two sides of their brains, via the corpus callosum - your own personal broadband. This is called 'whole-brain thinking'.*
>
> *1. Are you a left or right-brain thinker? Think about a difficult situation and how your brain handled it - was it logical (left) or creative (right)?*
>
> *2. Now use both brains - think in pictures and images too, not just in words, to dramatically increase your brain's output.*

2. Meditation can be a powerful information processing tool

The secret of meditation is to go out of your mind and not think of anything, starting with as little as five or ten minutes a day. It is paradoxical, that the less we think, the more powerful our thoughts become; in meditation the idea is to try to stop the thoughts completely. Stop the internal dialogue and you can hear the Eurekas!

Take time out to:

1. Set clear goals in every area of your life - write them down now:

-
-
-
-
-

2. Meditate every day as much as you can, and even more.

3. Visualise information to achieve your goals

The whole idea is to visualise as much as you can of each of your goals in as great a detail as possible. The secret is to use your 'imagination' and 'see' things happening in your mind's eye. The more 'information input', in the way of words, images, sounds or smells, that you can add to your visualisations, the better.

1. *Visualise as many things as you can that you want to happen in your life, including possible scenarios on how you achieved those things - note down a few ideas now:*

    •

    •

    •

    •

2. *Focus on doing things that you can do, not that others can do - remind yourself of them now:*

    •

    •

    •

    •

4. **Effective assimilation of information is key to building a competitive base of knowledge and expertise**

It is possible to assimilate huge amounts of information, without any stress. Being able to assimilate massive amounts of information very quickly helps enormously when you want to get up to speed very quickly on a particular subject or are carrying out a specific piece of research.

1. *Consider taking a course in speed reading - there are hundreds of options available.*

2. *When carrying out research, try to pick out using a highlighter pen, or onscreen highlighter, the key nuggets of information - do not rely on your memory, especially when going through large reports - mix it with pictures and then let go - relax, meditate, go for a walk.*

3. *Copy or remove these key information nuggets and place them in a summary document or folder for future reference.*

CHAPTER 11

PRESENTING INFORMATION EFFECTIVELY

"When presenting your information, they'll either get it or they won't - either way, it's up to you"

Ron G Holland

We have already established the one thing we are not short of is information. However, we are short of people who can present it in an articulate way that will elicit a desired response. In business, for example, this could be a critical decision to move a key project forward, the release of budget to fund a major marketing campaign or to make an acquisition.

Managing all the information assets you have effectively and sharing it with others is all fine and will drive value; however, there will come a time when you will either be asked to, or want to, present that information and the key insights, to a family gathering or important business meeting. Presenting to groups of people, strangely enough, is one of the most feared activities humans have - it comes ahead of our fear of snakes, heights or even death!

Of course, presenting information does not have to mean just 'face-to-face', in real time. There are many new media available today, allowing anyone to present, electronically, to a group of people - or even to a worldwide audience. These media don't require heavyweight investment in, for example, studio facilities, or radio or TV airtime, as they did in the past.

In this chapter we'll endeavour to establish what it is that master presenters and the Information Overlord do to meet these challenges; you will be better prepared to present information - and wow your audience at the same time!

Present to a stockbroker so that he will actually raise money for you

When presenting information to a stockbroker, the first question that is asked is, "What's the story?" And, by this, they don't mean you have a leisurely hour or an hour and a half. What they mean is, "Tell me the salient points, the elevator pitch, in sixty to ninety seconds." To make this work, boy, do you have to be prepared. The reason why they want a story that can be told in sixty to ninety seconds is that, when you have left the building and they decide to raise the money for your project, the senior broker gets all his brokers in a room and gives them a brief of what information to tell their clients over the phone. Guess what? Each phone call to each client is 60 to 90 seconds, "Hi Jon, have I got a deal for you! New stock I want to tell you about, an IPO. Yada, yada, yada, blah, blah, blah. OK great, I can count you in for £50K at 37p a share, thanks Jon." The broker hangs up the phone and he's on to the next 90-second call.

Let me give you an example. When Bruce Snyder, my business partner of 25 years, was preparing for the flotation of *Applied Holographics*, he had a meeting with a PR guy by the name of Ian James, a good friend of mine. Ian asked Bruce all about holograms and Bruce gave him the whole nine yards, rambling away for at least an hour on how holography could be used for decorating paper, Christmas cards, collectables, trading cards, watch dials, head-up displays on fighter aircraft, measuring defects in jet engines, and on and on and on. Somewhere in the course of the conversation, Bruce inadvertently slipped in that holograms could be used as a cost-effective security device that could be used on credit cards, bank notes, concert tickets and all legal documents. Suddenly Ian James snapped out of the 'hypnotic trance' that Bruce had put him in.

Ian had his 'story' and told Bruce to drop everything but the 'security aspect' of his hologram business. Between the two of them, they created a brilliant 'story' about "how this new cost-effective security device would bring counterfeiters to their knees and save the banking industry billions." He went on to procure a successful fundraising. The shares went from 5p to £6.80 and Bruce had over a million of them. He made out like a bandit. A bandit!

One final point is that my good friend, Neal Lyster, who I go back with many years, always calls the important information, "Assailant points" instead of "Salient points". When I asked him why, he simply replied, "Assailant points knock their socks off!"

The Business card that brings in business

I put it out into the ether that I would meet a very special business guru by the name of Sri Guruji Pillau, because I intuitively knew I could learn a lot from this man. I was doing some consultancy work in Belgium, staying at a friend's house and the phone rang. "Ron," said my friend Gisela, "it's for you." This was Frederick, a mutual friend of ours, and he had heard I was staying at Gisela's house for a few days. "What are you doing this afternoon, Ron? I have a house guest staying here by the name of Sri Guruji Pillau. He has seen all your books and audios on my coffee table and has requested a meeting with you. Would you like to come over and meet with him?" I had gently put this out to the universe, now I was about to meet my favourite guru; spooky or what?

On the trip over to downtown Brussels, I had many ideas go through my mind together with all the questions I would ask Sri. Once Gisela and I arrived and sat down at Frederick's coffee table, I was ready to ask hundreds of questions. However, it was not to be. Sri had what seemed like an invisible connection to my brain; he answered every single question that I had thought of asking - and lots more besides - without me saying a single word. Sri talked for over three hours, but the gem I want to share with you is what he said about business cards, and I think it's quite profound:

"Ron, many times folk do not realise all they need is a simple business card to create massive success. The secret is getting just the right information onto just the right card, to elicit the response you are seeking, and nothing more. Choose a nice, firm, good quality card; make sure you have your name and address and phone and email address, website and all other relevant contact details in a reasonable size print - so that when people are trying to phone you, they don't have to squint to read the small print. Make sure you have a maximum of three magic words clearly embossed on the card, announcing exactly what you do: Venture Capital Alternative, Corporate Financier, Information Overlord, Social Media Expert, Search Engine Optimisation, Internet Fraud & Security or whatever..."

I have now managed to get this information down to one word on my own card: Mentor.

Sri continued,

"Also make sure that if you change your phone number or any other information, do not scribble it out and then write on the back of the card. There is nothing less professional. Invest in new cards, so the image you portray is the best it can be at the time. The recipient of the card may not see your house, car, office or other accoutrements but they will get this information from the card as to who and what you are. You only get one chance to make a first impression and first impressions are very difficult to change!"

From the stage, grab people's attention in the first thirty seconds

I'm a great believer in grabbing the attention of my audience within the first 30 seconds; that doesn't happen by accident. Many times, obviously according to the audience and the subject, I'll begin with, "I don't know exactly how many millionaires I helped create - but it's a lot!"

I may then quickly follow that up with a few real-life examples, and then go on to explain that we'll be exploring many more during the day. Of course, the examples that I have chosen are from a very similar background and profession that my audience is from - I will have studied every single pre-workshop questionnaire that I send out with great diligence, to ensure that the information I am delivering is *exactly what they want to hear*. I make sure the stage is set up just how I like it, with copious supplies of water and the PA system is working perfectly. Nothing is worse than getting up on a new stage prepared to blow people away in the first 30 seconds - and your voice comes over all squeaky or not at all.

I use tonality and make sure that I deliver with great confidence, charisma and enthusiasm. Even these days, I mentally rehearse my opening gambit over and over again so I that I can actually feel that I have the audience in the palm of my hand. On the day, it goes down just like the mental rehearsal that I visualised. Just remember this, it's not *what* you say, it's the *way* that you say it.

Audio is all about tonality, sound effects and emotions

When we promoted my box set of self-help audio products in *Little Chef*'s up and down the country, we gathered together thousands of names and phone numbers of people who had bought the products and filled in the clip coupon requesting our bumper FREE gift. We set about doing market research to see how much our customers enjoyed the information on the audios and how many times they listened to each of them. We were amazed to hear that the customers listened to each audio an average of 30 times - wow! Let me tell you a little about what went into create an audio product that has now had a shelf life of over 20 years - and no signs of sales abating. We had the audios professionally produced in a big recording studio and had a producer and music people on hand. We used sound effects, sound bites and voice-over guys who narrated the text of the books; I came on live and did some pretty dynamic stories, interviews and vignettes. A lot of thought went into each 90-minute recording.

I wonder how many people reading this book remember the hilarious Kenny Everett show that ran on *BBC Radio One, Capital Radio* and *Victory Radio* in the seventies? Kenny often used to take the whole week making his one-hour show in his home recording studio, coming up with ridiculous stunts, hilarious gags, outrageous quips and the rudest, funniest, most quirky sound effects that he would painstakingly secure from the most unimaginable places. His attention to detail was inexhaustible. Despite most people's attention span being only seven minutes, Kenny used to attract his audience back, week after week, for his most brilliant one-hour show. To see how clever he was at keeping his followers attentive and amused, catch him on YouTube now.

Hopefully what you will have gleaned from the foregoing is that the information you are trying to impart to your audience is the easy bit. Presenting that information in an acceptable format, that is understood, appreciated, interesting and good enough to be listened to over and over again, takes not only time *and* hard work but *also* creativity *and* imagination.

YouTube and video that will be watched all the way through

Google is substantially the biggest and most effective search engine in the world - it is also the world's largest advertising agency. Google owns YouTube and it won't be long before folk automatically put their searches into YouTube first because there you will find a video *and* audio of all the information they are seeking. It's only a matter of time; when there is enough critical mass on YouTube to cover all the topics people are likely to search for, it will become the search engine of choice.

Video is the future of information and it is imperative that you get to grips with the medium. You can convey a powerful message within seconds; television advertising has been doing just that for years. YouTube has levelled the playing field and it allows anyone to get up their visual message and information quickly and cost effectively.

Over the past couple of years, we have learned a lot about video, the medium and video marketing. I'll share a few things from a personal perspective. We have learned that three to four minutes run time, per video, is the optimum; we frequently post new videos, to keep the message fresh. We use many different backdrops, not just those showing all my books, for example. I usually have a bullet-pointed script, with a large typeface, and have that hanging from the camera, at eye level, so I don't have to keep looking down at notes. I use tonality, enthusiasm and charisma to deliver my short message with punch - and I use Mike, my Bulgarian apprentice, as the 'fashion police' and he always makes sure that I am looking my best!

In three short minutes, I make sure my information contains tips, wisdom, real useable knowledge; I try hard to get over my message using tonality, wit, humour and fun. I also work on being memorable and make sure that my audience has my phone number, email address and a call to action - and I tell them I am expecting to see them again soon. We are really getting to grips with the medium and are now beginning to see demonstrable results in the way of more mentoring clients requiring this additional service - so much so that we have now set up our own 'green room' and are doing video marketing for other small businesses - cool, eh?

Websites that grab people by presenting the information they want

Stop and think for a moment - ask yourself how many websites you have landed on and then left very rapidly. Hundreds, perhaps even thousands? There is only one valid reason for you doing this; the specific information that you were seeking was either not there or, more likely, not presented in an easy-to-find way. We need to learn from this and act accordingly when presenting to our target audience using the World Wide Web; when people come across your message they will act quite ruthlessly if it does not immediately resonate with them.

The information that you have on your website has to be clear and uncluttered - and should not try to be all things to all men. You need to be your own severest critic, but also get feedback from your friends and family, work colleagues and, most importantly, your clients or customers. Carry out a simple 'usability' survey and then act on the feedback; I find this, nine times out of ten, to be very useful - free consultancy! People are invariably happy to tell you what they don't like.

Ensure that you have very clear buttons, menus and maps that allow your customers to access specific information, within the blink of an eye. Try to make use of the site intuitively - something which, judging by the huge number of very poor sites out there, is obviously extremely difficult to do. The heuristics, or roughly 'user friendliness', is something that can so easily be got wrong - and just as easily got right! Be consistent. Don't suddenly switch between buttons on the left and then buttons on the right -

keep them in the same place! If you are seeking opinions, don't change between scales of one to five where one is excellent - and then suddenly have a scale where five is excellent. Use the same colour scheme or typeface for the same thing throughout the site. The list of things you can get wrong is endless; these annoy users, and you don't want angry would-be clients!

Here's an example: my bank just changed their site around; it has been pretty good up to now. On the new site, it took me over an hour to find out where the statements are - instead of the sign that had been there for the past 10 years saying, 'view statements' which is pretty clear, cool and intuitive. I now have to click on my username. I wasted a whole hour but I also know this was not my fault. I eventually found it by getting into the mind of the programmer and asking myself, "Now if I were a complete idiot and had to hide 'view statements' where absolutely no one in their right mind would ever think of looking, where would I hide them?" Then I had an 'aha' moment, look for 'view statements' under your user name, and sure enough with one click up, they came. It took me an hour of searching around the site and some people believe that I am reasonably intelligent. I am absolutely sure the designer never asked any customers, did any beta testing, or got any feedback. He or she probably wrote this software in an office that is so busy that people don't have time to think any more.

This is not what Ted Nelson had in mind - at all. Remember Ted's rule about newcomers to a site finding information in 10 seconds flat - even in an emergency? Believe me, presenting information is an art *and* a science - and not everyone can do it.

Slide presentations that actually work

PowerPoint is an extremely powerful tool for delivering information to an audience. It is ideal for everything from sales talks and pitches to academic lectures - but unfortunately most people still overcomplicate it, because they fail to think it through in pragmatic terms.

Many PowerPoint presentations are shown on laptops in meetings at hotels and other transitory locations; if this is the case for you, you should be thinking carefully about how long you have got to make the presentation. If the meeting is in the coffee bar or lobby of a hotel, you should be thinking in terms of a total of 30 minutes - and no more than 45 minutes maximum. People generally have a sustained attention span of only 20-minute 'chunks' (children far less than this), so bear this in mind when creating natural pauses or breaks in your presentation.

Don't forget there will probably be some preamble, introductions, ordering coffee, even before you boot up your laptop. The person you are presenting the information to may very well have other meetings to get to, or trains or planes to catch. The last thing you want to be doing is missing out slides, or having to speak too quickly, to get through everything. Think all this through before you begin to create your slide show; it will pay dividends.

When it comes to making your slides, think in terms of fifteen slides maximum. Usually, 'less is more' - particularly with the time restraints we have just discussed. Make sure you have no more than five bullet points on each slide; and also remember that each slide should be no more than an aid memoire for you to start talking. If you address each bullet point for only 30 seconds, a 15-slide show with five bullets on each slide will still take you 37 and a half minutes to get through. This will allow you 10 minutes preamble and 10 minutes answering questions, closing or and setting up the next meeting with your prospect. An hour for a first business meeting is not uncommon; you may be able to turn it into 90 minutes; but don't forget we have not discussed whether your prospect wants to discuss something with you, or show you a presentation of his or her own. It takes a lot of skill and practice to be able to articulate a bullet point in 30 seconds, but this is part of the magic of delivering information effectively. When I was meeting people in hotel lobbies, I used to alert them, prior to the meeting, over the phone or by email, that I had a formal presentation to share with them that would take 40 minutes, and would this allow enough time to cover all other matters as well? Once I had established this was OK, it was a lot more relaxed and I could present my information with ease. It is always good to establish, at the beginning of a meeting at the latest, just how long it could last - does your host/client/prospect have any specific time by which they must finish? As already indicated, there's nothing worse than finding out, 10 minutes from the end (but 30 minutes before you were planning on finishing) that your contact has to move on.

Just a few more tips on PowerPoint presentations to help you on your way to becoming an Information Overlord: PowerPoint defaults to Arial and Times New Roman for a reason: they are easy to read. You can, of course, spend time being creative and playing around with other fonts -

but if you take my advice, you'll spend that time practising delivering 30 seconds' worth of brilliant content for each bullet point. By the way, PowerPoint has a tool for timing this. If you go to: **Slide Show, Rehearse Timings**, a small timing bar displays the total lapsed time, and the time for the current slide, in the top left-hand corner of the screen.

The content needs to be sharp and articulate and have a start, middle and ending; it should take the listener through a logical train of thought that explains things in sufficient detail, such that they won't have too many questions to ask at the end. The whole idea is to *anticipate* any questions and thoroughly answer them in the presentation of your information.

In one of our current presentations, which is for a business opportunity, we refer to various brochures, manuals and products throughout the PowerPoint presentation; we have these to hand to show as we talk through each bullet point. Having visual aids like this really cements and brings the presentation to life.

If used effectively, PowerPoint presentations will win you friends and help get you to that all-important decision-making moment that you are looking for from your manager, client or financier. There are hundreds of references on the Internet to things that you should avoid, though, when using PowerPoint. My favourites are:

- Limit the use of animations and effects: they can dilute the message you are trying to get across.
- Be consistent with the use of colours, fonts, positions of text, bullets, etc.

- Pictures can really help bring colour, life and example to presentations - but just be careful only to use them where they create impact and not just as 'wallpaper'.

- Black backgrounds with white copy may look very impactful on screen - but when it comes to printing out, clients or customers will not thank you for the amount of ink or toner that the slides gobble up.

- Avoid busy or complicated background templates - your message will very quickly get lost in the detail.

- Slide handouts can be great for people to have while you are presenting, however it does mean that they can jump to the end of your presentation before you do! Better to advise your audience that handouts will be distributed at the end.

- Be careful when trying to embed videos as they can really slow down your laptop and sometimes not run at all when they need to, especially if you have to transfer your presentation to a corporate laptop linked in to their display system. I prefer using links to videos stored on YouTube or a Cloud server - but these depend on having a reliable Internet connection.

- Avoid 'joke' slides - unless you are a qualified comedian!

Dream brochure and lift sheet

In my mentoring and consultancy practice, we have to make many presentations to procure debt and equity funding, to engage non-executive directors who invest and to secure many everyday skills, resources and needs that my clients have and haven't been able to get elsewhere.

Over the years we have developed a four-page full-colour glossy brochure. It is A3 folded in half, giving four sheets of A4 to present all the information we need.

Each sheet is dominated by pictures; the whole idea is to present a storyboard of information of where we are, where we are going and what we need to get there. Each picture carries a short caption. Inside the four-pager we slip in an A4 lift sheet that is carefully set out on 100gm paper. It contains contact details, directors' information, the amount of money we are seeking and any relevant business information - in particular, making a point of what's in it for them! If it won't fit on one side of A4, we leave it out. Obviously the contact details are also on the four-pager as well, should they ever get separated.

The whole thing can be viewed by a tired investor, broker, non-executive, lawyer or accountant or anyone else we are trying to attract the attention of, on the train or on the way home. Ideally the information will be presented in such a clear, powerful and exciting way that it will have the reader's tongue hanging out for more, and force them to ask the question, "Is there a business plan for this?" or "Can we meet the team?" or preferably, "Who do I make the cheque payable to?" Once you have grabbed their attention, there will be plenty of time for reading boring, photocopied business plans that are all curling up at the edges.

The secret is to grab people's attention with minimal but well-thought-through and well-prepared information; allowing their imaginations and emotions to do most of the work for you.

Making a formal presentation

Sometimes you have to make formal presentations where no enthusiasm, humour or motivation is apparently required, just the facts. In these instances, I still use enthusiasm, tonality and humour - but toned down a tad to get the presentation on to a professional level. I also really believe that a *passion* for the subject being presented is critical to making a presentation a success, even when taking place in these circumstances.

It really pays dividends to understand your audience. Do they know less or more than you? You may be presenting to a bunch of students, in which case your knowledge will far exceed theirs; on the other hand, you may be presenting to a board of governors or teachers - in that case it is highly likely their knowledge will outweigh your own.

If you are presenting to people who know *less* than you, make the subject interesting, not too highbrow and rule out any ambiguities. Often, less is more. Many times you *will* stretch your audience and when you do, it is nice to really articulate what you are describing, maybe using graphs, illustrations or even cartoons. It is lovely when a student says, "Do you know what? This is the first time I have ever heard it put like that; now I know what it means, how it works and what to do about it. Thank you!" I have heard that kind of comment literally hundreds of times throughout my career and it is very rewarding.

When presenting to people whose level of subject knowledge is far *greater* than yours, all you have to do is show them the exact state of understanding that you have about the topic that you are going to present. What impresses most is if you can actually demonstrate you understand the subject on a practical level and have really grasped it, not just on a superficial, intellectual level.

People and your audience will process information in three main ways, and we each tend to have an innate preference for one or the other:

- **Pictures and images** - in other words, visual representation of information. 'Visual' people will be trying to convert all your ideas into images as you deliver your presentation

- **Words and sounds** - Auditory people will quickly pick up on ambiguities, inconsistencies or anything illogical. Everything you say to them must 'sound' right

- **Feelings, emotions and, sometimes, 'tactile'** - these individuals will often go inside themselves to make sure what you are saying 'feels right'

Understanding and empathising with the way your audience is 'translating' and emotionally responding to your presentation is a key skill that you should endeavour to acquire. It will pay significant dividends every time you stand up in front of a group of people.

Body Language

I have talked a lot about the tools and techniques that the Information Overlord will use to transform what might be relatively boring 'static' information into a presentation that will delight and surprise his audience. These tools and techniques, however, will fall on deaf ears unless you also adhere to a rigorous body language regime each and every time you present to an important audience.

> **Body language** - how you look, how you come across - accounts for a significant part of a presentation's impact:

How it is said - **50%**

BODY LANGUAGE - **30%**

Visual aids - **12%**

Content - **8%**

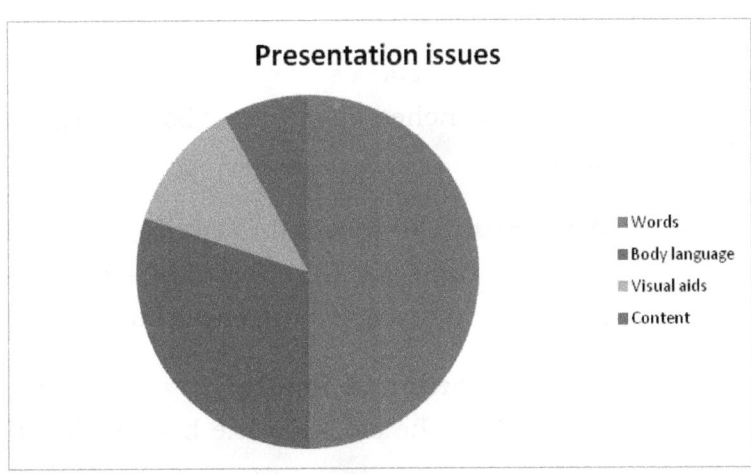

Here are the body language and presentational techniques that really work for me:

- **Dress appropriately:** Wear something that both you and your audience will be comfortable with.

- **Eye contact:** The minute your audience enters the room, greet them with a handshake (if appropriate) and one-to-one eye contact, as this will immediately instil confidence and trust in you, the presenter.

- **Maintain good eye contact:** Do this throughout the presentation, but do not dart from person to person.

- **Smile and look motivated:** Positive energy will be picked up by the people around the table - carry this through to the tone of voice you use. Remember, we previously mentioned that 'passion sells'.

- **Keep your distance:** Stand at least seven feet away from your audience.

- **Keep your balance:** When standing still, keep feet a few inches apart, your body weight evenly balanced.

- **Don't rush:** Use pauses throughout the presentation to create audience 'thinking time' - never rush as this will be translated into frenetic body language.

- **Speak clearly and loudly:** A good tip is always to 'speak to the clock on the back wall'. There's not much worse than those at the back not being able to hear you.

- **Learn how to use the microphone:** Depends on the size of the room, but if you have one, find out how to speak into it - some need a voice very close to the device, some will pick your voice up from a distance away.

- **Control nerves:** We all get these from time to time - practise beforehand, as this will help avoid embarrassment on the day. Avoid holding a glass or papers - these may exaggerate any trembling or nervousness.

- **Don't over-gesture:** Using your hands to 'animate' is fine, preferably by using your open palms - but be careful not to over-use. Otherwise keep them by your side, below waist level.

- **Don't appear aggressive:** Walking towards a seated audience whilst talking can make some people feel quite uncomfortable.

- **Don't appear aloof:** The 'royal' hands held behind your back can often give this impression.

Making informal presentations

In business, we are making informal presentations to our colleagues and managers all the time, often without even realising it. Every time you are called into the marketing manager's office or having an impromptu meeting with the accountant, be prepared to use your presentation techniques to create the best impact and get the result you want from the situation.

I have always found that, by simply taking in a pen and paper, my diary and possibly a calculator, I feel more prepared and ready to answer any questions thrown at me. Body language here is also important. Always use good eye contact, never slouch and act professionally at all times. Doing all of these things will place you in a more assertive position, ready to take on whatever is asked of you.

When presenting to very senior management, remember the 'less is more' rule. I have found that CEOs, in particular, require very little background numbers or statistics - they will expect all this work to have been done by you behind the scenes. What they want to see is the insight from the work you have carried out and more importantly, what that means as an opportunity or risk limiter for the business going forward. To get this type of message across, I have found pictures, the odd graph and a small number of strategically placed words work best. CEOs will be thinking about the *bigger picture* - not necessarily the fine detail behind the presentation.

How car salesmen and closers present information

Master car salespeople either know these powerful techniques intuitively or have learned them along the way. What the top-flight salesperson will do is share his or her information in a conversational manner, all the time picking up clues, on both a conscious and subconscious level, to see what parts of the presentation the prospects show enthusiasm for. They will lead by trying to elicit a response about the colour, shape and design of the car, deliberately pointing out minute design detail such as the rear view mirror and design of the instrument panel, to see if the potential customer is 'biting'. He or she may then lead on to the 'sound' of the engine, the exhaust note and the doors closing, to see if that grabs their attention. Finally they will let the customers get the 'feel' of the car by letting them drive it and see if it 'feels' OK. "Are the seats comfortable for you? How does the car feel on the road? Do you like the steering geometry? Can you feel the aerodynamic shape cutting through the air?"

When I first started out in sales, I used to think that these old sales guys were daft going through all these routines until I started to study their track records and sales figures. I soon got the gist of it and was hitting auditory, visual and kinaesthetic cues and closing deals myself. Like one top-notch closer told me, "What's the point in rambling on about visual information about the colour, design and shape when all the guy wants to know is auditory information about all the 'sounds' of the car in order to complete his decision-making process?"

ZOOM SECRETS

Your Personal Action Plan (11)

1. It is imperative to grab people's attention in the first 30 seconds of a presentation or sales pitch

Get to know what makes your audience tick and what will turn them on - understand their needs. If running a seminar, study every single pre-workshop questionnaire with great diligence. Ensure that the information presented is exactly what they want to hear. Use tonality and **deliver with great confidence, charisma and enthusiasm.**

Always mentally rehearse a presentation opening over and over again, to the point where you see the audience in the palm of your hand. Remember, it's not what you say, it's the way that you say it.

 1. Create a short sentence now that will captivate your audience the minute you start speaking at your next presentation:

....
....
....

2. What are your audiences needs/wants? Note down a few thoughts, ready for your next presentation or sales pitch:

-
-
-

3. Do not waffle or try to confuse your audience with words or numbers from the outset - this will turn them off!

2. Use video to get your message across to the masses - globally

Video is the future of information. It can convey a powerful message within seconds. YouTube allows anyone to publish their visual message and information quickly and cost effectively, from almost anywhere and without air time restrictions. But remember:

1. *Only create powerful videos that people will want to watch.*

2. *Three to four minutes run time per video is the optimum to get your message across without boring the viewer.*

3. *Regularly produce and publish new videos to keep your message fresh.*

4. *Always consider the backdrop to your video - get it wrong and the viewer will be distracted from what you are saying.*

5. *Prepare a written large typeface bullet-pointed script and make sure it is easy to read and not in view of the camera.*

6. *When speaking, use tonality, enthusiasm and charisma to deliver your message with punch.*

7. Consider carefully what you are wearing - image still counts for a lot these days.

8. Try and incorporate a 'call to action' at the end of your video - information with value should create an action or decision.

9. If you want feedback or an order placed, do not forgot to include your contact details.

3. **Really effective websites will grab people's attention by presenting the information they need and want**

A website can be a significant source of direct or indirect revenue if constructed well and if the information provided adds value to the reader's online experience. Content should be clear, uncluttered and engaging and should not try to be all things to all men.

1. *Be your own severest critic - note down five things that you are not 100% happy with on your current website:*

   -
   -
   -
   -
   -

2. Get feedback from your friends and family, work colleagues and, most importantly, your clients or customers - note down five names of people you will be approaching:

   -
   -
   -
   -
   -

3. Carry out simple 'usability' testing, both by yourself and friends - try to break the site, test all links etc. - then ACT on the results.

   - Ensure all buttons, menus and maps are clear and intuitive to use.

   - Check for 'user friendliness' - something that is often overlooked.

   - Get feedback on style and design - does it reflect your business vision or brand positioning?

4. Slide presentations can be a valuable resource and work hard for you

Used effectively, PowerPoint presentations will help get you to that all-important decision-making moment. Get it wrong though and it really can be 'death by PowerPoint' for your audience.

Remember:

1. *Limit the use of animations and effects.*

2. *15 slides is the optimum for a typical presentation that will hold people's attention span.*

3. *Be consistent with the use of colours, fonts, positions of text, bullets, etc.*

4. *Pictures can help bring colour, life and example - be careful only to use them where they create impact and not just as 'wallpaper'.*

5. *Black backgrounds with white copy may look very impactful on screen but are not ideal for printing out.*

6. *Avoid busy or complicated background templates.*

7. *Embedded videos can slow down your laptop or sometimes not run at all - use links to videos instead if you have access to a network server or the Internet.*

8. *Avoid 'joke' slides - unless you are a qualified comedian!*

5. Body language accounts for 30% of a presentations impact

This fact is probably a big surprise to the novice presenter. All other tools and techniques that might be deployed during a presentation will fall on deaf ears if proper attention and rigorous focus is not given to the use of body language by the presenter.

Be prepared and get your act together:

1. *Watch training videos, read articles and practice with colleagues and experts.*

2. *Research body language training videos on YouTube - there are almost 70,000!*

3. *Body language can play a key role in closing a sale - remain relaxed and empathise with your customer both in body stance and verbal response.*

CHAPTER 12

CREATING SUSTAINABILITY INTELLIGENTLY AND GLOBALLY

"Sustainability should be the primary quest of humanity in the twenty-first century"

Ron G Holland

I am restraining myself from launching straight into sustainability, not because it is vast, global, complicated and topical - but primarily because it is also a highly emotive subject, one that needs careful consideration and due diligence. It is also one that offers huge commercial opportunities, but only for those who have really done the research and got their minds around the real essence of sustainability and its associated complexities. I hope that it has become apparent that, as an Information Overlord, above everything else, you have started to see that *you really have to do your own thinking*. As a business guru and mentor, this is even more crucial and as I have stated on many occasions, it's no good patting each other on the back as we dive over the precipice. However, when it comes to the whole arena of sustainability, we have to go even further in the diligent way we approach our research. That's why I want to introduce you to...

Confirmation Bias

The term 'Confirmation bias' was coined by the outstanding English psychologist Peter Wason who was Cambridge educated and passed away in 2003. No book on information would be complete without having, at least, a brief discussion about the term. Confirmation bias is a tendency for people to favour information that confirms their own beliefs. You can see how dangerous this is, especially when those beliefs are charged with emotion. Lots of experiments have been conducted that suggest people carrying out research will focus their attention toward confirming their existing beliefs, even to the exclusion of all alternatives. The Information Overlord cannot afford to let this happen, not just in relation to sustainability, but for any research subject that he or she undertakes.

Whilst a third of the globe is slowly but surely getting focused on *sustainability*, another third of the world is focused on *success at any cost,* playing catch up and trying to attain some of the wealth, accoutrements and lifestyle that the western world has enjoyed for decades. The other third, nearly three billion people, is trying hard to *survive at no cost* on $2 day and don't concern themselves with Internet access - or anything else for that matter, unless it's edible. We must not forget the impact the two-thirds are having on global affairs, as we strive to become sustainable, because the population is far from being on an equal playing field. Although Africans account for 14% of the global population, they only make up 1.7% of global Internet users. China will retain its current position as the leading global consumer of coal, building new power stations at an alarming rate, even as it endeavours to diversify. Bread or computers still need to be taken into the equation.

Definition of sustainability

There has been a lot written about the definition of sustainability - I suspect too much, because things start to become complicated and then no one really knows what to focus on. I am a great believer in 'articulate simplicity', and if, over the next five, ten or fifteen years, you lose your way, come back to this simple definition of sustainably. As succinctly as I can put it: *it is the capacity to endure and be able to maintain at a fixed level without exhausting natural resources or damaging the environment.*

Sustainability, global warming and Information Technology

There is an intrinsic link between sustainable development, sustainable growth or just sustainability and global warming. It is impossible to talk about these highly complex subjects without bringing them altogether and, in a way, that is where the problem begins. The intelligent Information Overlord has to take on a holistic approach - and that view is inevitably very large indeed. It takes a brave soul to be talking to a conservation group about printing on both sides of a sheet of paper, not to print emails and switch the lights off, all in order to conserve - when you know there is a country the other side of the world opening a brand new fossil-fuel-driven power station every single day of the year.

Over the past 150 years, industrialised nations have unwittingly upset the delicate balance of nature, which is called 'homeostasis', by burning inordinate amounts of carbon-producing fossil fuels, building millions of gas-guzzling vehicles, breeding vast numbers of methane-producing livestock and cutting down swathes of carbon-digesting rain forests. We have already witnessed devastating results of global warming: the tragic tsunami in Indonesia on Boxing Day 2004 that claimed over 300,000 lives, the unforgettable wipe-out of New Orleans and the near-catastrophic nuclear disaster in Japan caused by a tsunami in 2011. It is not surprising that the layman, including me and many within the IT industry, would jump to the conclusion that the above activities were, in a big way, partly to blame for the disasters of the past and the many that are highly likely to happen in the future.

However, after much non-biased research I discovered the truth is much nearer to home - and possibly even more unpalatable, if that could possibly be so. In actual fact it's the number of 'computer farms' and individual computers and the IT industry as a whole that is in part to blame for using vast amounts of power to drive and cool its global operations.

The good news is that many of the leaders at the top end of the industry have recognised this fact and are now working hard to develop semi-conductor chips that create much less heat and also take a lot less cooling. Leaders are trying to reduce power consumption of entire networks, including data-centres, by 30% and reduce power consumption of individual computers by a whopping 50%. Obviously they are doing lots of other things as well and we'll cover a few of them a little later.

Much of the IT industry is now embarking on a highly sophisticated two-pronged approach to massively reduce power consumption and hence global carbon emissions. They are very carefully analysing and then implementing ideas that can make the overall IT industry much more energy efficient, especially by implementing virtualisation. At the same time they are looking to see how they can help other industries reach optimum levels of energy efficiency as well as helping lesser-developed countries grow and develop in a sustainable way, without damaging the environment. The industries that are being targeted in the first phase are logistics, energy management, motor controllers, private transport and building design.

Sustainable development is often an overused word, and in some instances has even become a buzzword, but the Information Overlord must bear in mind that over a billion people globally exist at poverty level with no running water or access to any other basic necessities. Creating sustainability is a massive challenge; however, it is one that we are well-suited to embrace.

An interesting footnote: 40% of France's primary energy is non-polluting nuclear power and Brazil is already producing 50% of its power from renewable energy.

Virtualisation

Various technologies known as *virtualisation* have come to rescue the IT industry. Virtualisation technologies allow more efficient and cost-effective management of IT resources, which also results in lowering power consumption. So what is it? You build a few powerful servers and install on them a large number of 'virtual' computers. They are virtual, because they run as software on those powerful physical computers; however, when you connect to them via a network (such as the Internet) you have no way of knowing if it is a physical or virtual computer - and, even if you could tell them apart, it makes no difference to you anyway! The software managing the virtual environment allocates physical resources to the virtual computer dynamically, depending on the load. Most computers are idle for most of the time, so their resources can be allocated to those that require them at a given time - that's why you can run 100 virtual computers on five to ten physical ones. Would that be useful in your organisation?

So, virtualisation allows you to run a large number of computers on very little hardware (only a few physical computers). If the demand on resources increases beyond its capacity, you simply add another physical computer and move a few virtual computers to the new one seamlessly, with no downtime. Also, if one physical computer fails, the other ones in the cluster will take over and run the virtual computers from the one that failed. Virtualisation not only saves costs, but also speeds up maintenance tremendously - what used to take a few days, now can be done in a few minutes, and sometimes even seconds, and most of it can be automated. Virtualisation saves electricity, costs of buying new hardware, space for hardware, IT support time, maintenance cost and downtime. It's the miracle of the twenty-first century IT world.

Profit versus Sustainability

Moore's law states that that the speed of computers doubles every two years and so far, for around 50 years, this has proved to be true. Moore was a co-founder of Intel and he first discussed this mind-blowing revelation in a paper in 1965. Since then, another executive at Intel, David House, has been quoted as saying, "the speed doubles every 18 months."

While you pick your jaw up off the floor, you may want to consider what implications that has for information production and management, sustainability and profits. In simple terms, it means that you could, quite realistically, hang onto your computer for an extra year, perhaps even two or three, without considering an expensive upgrade that will ultimately consume more materials and resources and cause more landfill. However, business just doesn't work like that; there is an ever-increasing demand, backed up by a billion-dollar advertising campaign, for you to upgrade and keep up to date with all the mouth-watering technological gadgets and advances. Anyone can see that what is needed, and indeed called for, is hardware that is re-usable and *simply* upgradable to take it to the next level of processing capability; ultimately that product should be 100% recyclable.

Of course, what we are talking about here far transcends what is happening in computer hardware. It happens in just about everything in every industry and that is what the Information Overlord needs to be vitally aware of. It is yet another one of those things that lends itself to the massive commercial opportunity that will come out of the 'sustainably' era. Let's take one more example:

Electric and hybrid cars and trucks

Creeping up on us almost silently, literally and figuratively, are the electric vehicles of the future that bring with them some daunting challenges - as well as some awesome business opportunities. The businesses and entrepreneurs that can see the 'big picture' and not fall foul of 'confirmation bias' will ultimately reap the biggest rewards.

There are a number of problems however that need to be addressed. Current battery technology still falls way short of allowing meaningful long distance travel. Even a 'fast charge' takes two hours and I can't imagine too many car owners sitting around at service stations awaiting the batteries to charge, knowing full well that they can only get another 50 miles before they have to go through whole thumb-twiddling procedure again. There has to be a way of replacing these heavy batteries en route; quickly, cleanly and safely and, above everything else, cost effectively. Manufacturers will need to get their minds around a battery of one shape and size to allow this to happen - currently they are miles apart, creating a rod for their own backs. Just as happened in the world of information technology, video recording and, more recently, high definition DVDs, standards need to be applied - and fast.

Just as we are getting close to the point of 'total information overload', the UK national grid is also operating at close to full capacity. How will it cope when the number of electric vehicles on our roads matches that of petrol and diesel vehicles? To create a national grid that could supply electricity to run thirteen million cars on the roads of the UK alone, the grid would have to increase exponentially and I don't see any evidence of them starting just yet.

It doesn't take too much imagination to ponder upon the secret meetings and discussions that senior executives must be having in boardrooms, about the multi-billion dollar investments that they have made in motoring: internal combustion engine design, technology, plant and equipment, engineering and people; they'll also be wondering when is the right time to start mass producing a full range of hybrid or low-cost full-blown electric cars, rather than just the token gesture, expensive examples out there at the moment. Believe me, these secret meetings are still going on and already some manufactures have left it far too late.

The market in 'clean' transportation is already into the billions of dollars and expected to rise massively by 2020;

any manufacturer not having a sexy *and* viable line-up of electric cars by 2025 will be signing its own death warrant. Any government, state or council not getting to grips with the appropriate infrastructure will also be heading towards oblivion. Eventually, the viable electric vehicle age will reshape the energy grid, redefine driving patterns and generally improve the quality of life in urban areas - where most of the world's population will live and drive. IT systems will feature heavily, in guiding both the development and deployment of all clean transportation technologies.

Of course, it has to do with lots of things: correct information, timing, vision, technology, economics, belief, marketing intelligence, competition, public perception and many other things. Take the recent case of Kodak going into administration. It's beggars belief that no one on the board or no outside adviser ever said, "Look guys, digital is where it's all at. Let's use our brand, intellectual capital, profits, knowhow, resources - and set up a R&D facility that will focus just on digital cameras. Let's get ourselves ahead of the game. That's got to be better than playing Mr Ostrich."

It's clear for the world to see that this should not be allowed to happen in the transportation industry, as the stakes for the environment are so high. It will be interesting to see, however, which of the car manufacturers are going to play Mr Ostrich, which will be the early adopters and lose their shirts, and which will be the ones that get the timing just right and make billions. This is the conundrum; to paraphrase one of my all-time heroes, Winston Churchill, it is a riddle wrapped in a mystery inside an enigma.

Training and education

Did you ever stop to think how much energy it takes to send an email or click on a webpage? Probably not! Rick Zarr from Texas Instruments asked himself that very question and undertook a study with a team of researchers to find the answer.

They concluded that the average page request occupied about 315,000 bytes of data. That's 2.52×10^6 bits. The total energy required for the transaction was 4.6×10^{-6} joules per bit. Multiplying these two numbers result in 11.52 joules. We add in the server energy of 0.02 joules for a total of 11.61 watt-seconds (joules) for each page view. This is not streaming video, but a static webpage access from a server. If you now multiply that single access by one million every second (a medium city's population browsing the Web), you get an energy consumption number of around 11.610 kilowatts an hour to keep the data moving... enough energy to power roughly 13 US households for a month! For viewing 100 pages in a day, that would be about 323 milliwatt-hours of energy - or the equivalent of watching TV for about 10 minutes - an interesting thought. (*http://energyzarr.typepad.com/energyzarr nationalcom/2008/08/index.html*)

What about the energy used to carry out a simple Google information search? The view out there on the Internet is that a typical search generates about 7g of carbon dioxide (CO^2) - boiling a kettle generates about 15g. Google operates huge data centres around the world that consume a great deal of power, states Alex Wissner-Gross, a Harvard University physicist who has carried out research on the environmental impact of computing. In his view, a Google search has a definite environmental impact.

Every time you send out 140 characters over Twitter, how much energy do you think that consumes? According to some back-of-napkin calculations from Raffi Krikorian, a developer for Twitter's Platform Team, each tweet sent consumes about 90 joules. That means each tweet emits about 0.02 grams of CO_2 into the atmosphere, so roughly fifty million tweets sent on average per day delivers the equivalent of one metric ton of CO_2. To put this into perspective, about one metric ton of CO_2 is produced to meet the average monthly energy demand of the typical American household!

I truly believe that this type of knowledge sharing and training is the one area in which the Information Overlord can make an immediate, positive difference to the effect that information and information overload has on our environment. And it can be done cost effectively and, more often than not, actually lead to a net commercial benefit - whether it be at home or in the world of business. We all need to be trained in, fully understand and have a list of practical things we can easily action every day in order to lessen the negative effect that information production, dissemination and storage can have on our planet's resources.

There already exists a mammoth gap in the marketplace for plain-speaking sustainability information products, whether they are books, seminars, events or TV shows. Training and teaching at schools, colleges and business also needs to be ramped up. The dissemination of information about sustainability is going to be a major driving force in making the whole thing work, and this needs to happen not only from the top down, but from bottom up as well. Grass roots mobilisations will frequently lead the way when they eventually reach critical mass.

Information sustainability measures we can take in business

1. Create a sustainability champion

Nearly all of the top 150 companies in the world now have a full time Chief Sustainably Officer (CSO); in many instances this is a main board position, usually reporting directly to the CEO, but also forming a very good working relationship with the Chief Financial and Chief Marketing Officers. The appointment often proves to be very disruptive, but it is usually a seminal point in the company's history.

A good analogy would be to compare the post of a Chief Electricity Officer in the 1890s in some USA major companies, an appointment made to take advantage of the introduction of electricity. Those who got their minds around the transitions quickly capitalised on the multitude of opportunities that availed themselves when steam engines, electric generators and hydrowheels became obsolete. Those companies that had vision and had 'seen' the future jumped on the bandwagon and gained massive commercial advantage over their competitors.

The CSO will be expected, not just to integrate and navigate sustainability into the core strategy of the business, but also make the board aware of business opportunities, acquisitions, technologies and other ideas as they become apparent, in this now fast-moving arena. The CSO will also mobilise prefects, start education, initiate training, handle related communication and develop internal and external PR.

Major companies such as Siemens, GE, Marks & Spencer, Pepsi, Scottish Water, The Post Office and Philips are already creating billions in revenues from environmental, energy-efficient and green initiatives - both from a cost saving and consumer product perspective. The role of the CSO will, most likely, have been instrumental in bringing these successful initiatives to life.

2. Implement a few basic rules for employees and office managers

To many, this will all seem very mundane; however, as Information Overlords, we do need to consider the multiplier effect of hundreds of thousands of office managers or facilities managers who have yet to put sustainability processes in place. Literally tons of information is still being printed, whether it is emails, reports, spreadsheets - or just pictures of employees' holiday destinations! Massive number of printers will still be churning out in high-quality print mode, when 90% of the time low-quality will do. Server resources, storage space and energy will be wasted storing high resolution images, when a lower resolution is all that is really needed. Not only does all of this create problems for the environment, but it also adds significant overhead costs to the businesses letting it all happen.

- Make someone in your business responsible for reducing paper usage across the organisation.

- At the bottom of emails, include a line such as '*Think twice before printing*'.

- Install recycling points for paper, card, metal cans and ink cartridges.

- Compress and archive information files, reports, photographs etc.

- Unless essential, turn off computer hardware when the office is not occupied.

- Set printer defaults to 50% ink usage and double-sided (duplex) printing.

3. Implement videoconferencing facilities

Videoconferencing allows visual and audio communication between two or more locations and is just like being in the same room with the people you are having the conference with. You can share information on white boards and documents with ease. These days, with powerful computer processing coupled with video compression technology, you can have a quality conference between offices that could be thousands of miles apart in different countries, without the IT guy having to come in every five minutes to fix things. What's even better, these days, is that this sort of technology is available to anyone - anywhere - with a decent computer, a webcam, a Skype account and an Internet connection. You can avoid expensive business trips and save on wasted travel time, planes, trains, traffic jams, jet lag and airline food (which I happen to love) *and* reduce your carbon footprint at the same time. Microsoft, for example, claims to have, through videoconferencing alone, eliminated the equivalent of *100 million miles of air travel each year.* That's the equivalent of at least 4,000 trips around the world!

There have been calls in the past for larger businesses, globally, to install their own videoconferencing facilities as well as to create thousands of centres globally that individuals and smaller companies can access with ease and communicate visually with their counterparts. This would provide the catalyst for videoconferencing to become more mainstream and not just a luxury for those that can afford the hardware.

4.   Create efficient data centres

The forerunner of the data centre was the massive computer rooms that were built in the early stages of the computer industry. I remember, as a young but eager apprentice, being involved in the construction of one of these massive dust-free, air-conditioned rooms in the late sixties on Goodge Street in London. I would marvel at the massive mainframe computers, with their external tape drives whirring around, whilst *The Good, the Bad and the Ugly* boomed out of a tinny transistor radio in the background.

Fast-forward four decades and now Google has developed very efficient data centres and has created five simple steps for maximum efficiency that anyone can use. This information they share with the world:

- **Measure the PUE:** This is the key, and what energy efficiency is all about. PUE stands for Power Usage Effectiveness and simply means that if $20 worth of electricity comes into a data centre, as much of that as possible needs to be doing productive, profitable work - as opposed to merely running the servers themselves. Highly sophisticated measuring devices and meters are employed to measure this; once you know where energy is being used unnecessarily, you can take steps to counter this and increase efficiency.

- **Manage airflow:** Servers are highly sensitive to temperature and air flow; to operate at optimum efficiency, they must be kept at specific temperatures at all times. Google invested in everyday materials like sheet metal, meat locker screens and sheet metal doors to stop hot air mixing with cold air and ensuring it was flowing in the right direction.

- **Adjust the thermostat:** By allowing the temperature to increase from 23.3^0 Celsius to 26.6^0 Celsius, the manufacturers recommended operating temperature, even further efficiencies can be gained - most data centres tend to be over-cooled.

- **Utilise free cooling:** Google try hard to get as much free cooling as they can, by taking advantage of local conditions and harnessing ambient temperatures. Where possible, they also use sea water for cooling (and ensure that, when they empty that water back into the sea it, it has cooled right down.)

- **Optimise power distribution:** Google is always on a quest to improve efficiency and reduce power consumption. One of the innovative things they accomplished was to save electricity when power charges their massive standby batteries (that they have in case of power failure). Usually, the electricity has to be converted from AC into DC and then back to AC and then DC again.

Every time one of these conversions takes place, power is lost forever. What Google has managed to engineer is that the standby batteries are now connected directly to the servers, thereby removing the need for a number of the conversions, and thus minimising power loss.

5. Learn from the big boys

Even though the big players out there have a huge number of resources and an endless supply of funds to throw at sustainability, it does not mean that the Information Overlord cannot learn a thing or two for application elsewhere. I have picked out just a few examples of information-driven sustainability initiatives that I believe many organisations, as well as individuals, can learn from.

Facebook now has 30,000 servers and is still growing. It stores some 80 billion images and serves up 60,000 images a second. You may have picked up in the press that founder Mark Zuckerberg is a self-claimed hunter and sustainability enthusiast and is attempting to only eat meat that he kills himself. He has stated that, as a result of the experience, he is now eating a lot more healthily and has learned a lot about sustainable farming and the raising of animals.

Clearly Mark Zuckerberg is leading by example, which is the right way to go, but I wonder how many of Facebook's employees will take up the same approach to delivering sustainability within the Facebook organisation or in their homes? The good thing is that Zuckerberg has put in place many other initiatives to move his sustainability agenda forward. This includes appointing a sustainability team to champion the cause; it will also look closely at business process areas, such as the infrastructure supply chain, as well as developing the 'Open Compute Project' that aims to make data centres more sustainable through more efficient technology. Visit *http://opencompute.org/* for more information on this.

Apple is building America's largest solar farm on 100 acres of land in North Carolina, generating a massive 20 megawatts - helping power their operations, including iTunes. Apple is also now starting to use LED lighting to illuminate their stores around the world. In China, there is a photovoltaic solar park generating two hundred megawatts of power.

Microsoft has set itself a goal to reduce carbon emissions per unit of revenue by at least 30%, compared to 2007 levels. The company has put in place a flexible work-from-home policy, waste and recycling programmes - and commuting incentives, making it easier for employees to make greener choices. The company purchases renewable energy wherever it can, and has a code of social and environmental conduct that suppliers have to sign up to.

A common theme running throughout this chapter is the need to improve data centre efficiencies - in today's world, the home of information. Microsoft is no exception here and continues to optimise their centres, employ and help define green IT best practices, and use their own technology to improve operational efficiencies. Compared with data centres built just three years ago, new units are claimed to consume 50% less energy.

Sony has embraced the power of the populous and social media to lead a key environmental initiative. The company in 2010 launched its first-ever crowd-sourcing challenge, inviting ideas to create sustainable lifestyles from existing technologies. From hundreds of entries, judges selected volunteering mobile app '+U' which has been developed further through Sony's 'Open Planet Ideas' Facebook page.

HP has collaborated with the World Wildlife Fund (WWF) 'to combat climate change around the globe'. The partnership will see HP leveraging its technology innovation expertise to deliver environmental conservation in areas such as greenhouse gas emissions, impact on global forests, reduced energy consumption; it will also be showcasing IT solutions for a low carbon economy. As with Sony, HP has also harnessed 'people power' with their WWF 'Earth Hour campaign'; this has seen people in over 130 countries participate in turning off their lights for an hour on a day during March.

What all of these examples clearly show is that the businesses out there that market their information technology products to the likes of you and me are taking the issue of the environment very seriously. The ones that will make the biggest difference, in my opinion, are those that are directly engaging with their consumers and people around the world to multiply the power of the information sustainability initiatives they have developed. The Information Overlord can learn much from this!

Similar initiatives are mentioned in the movie *HOME*, which can be found on YouTube: *http://www.youtube.com/watch?v=jqxENMKaeCU*

Individual responsibility

It is paradoxical that, if we want to enjoy the considerable benefits of the 'information age', we need to examine every conceivable way of conserving energy. The infrastructure of the 'information highway' costs so much to run - not just in terms of money, but also many other resources that the world is slowly running out of. We are now living beyond the capacity of our planet, pumping out more CO_2 than the earth can absorb, using up resources quicker than they can be regenerated. If we continue this rate of consumption, by 2030 we would need two planets to sustain us!

At a micro level, individuals can come together as 'grass roots' organisations and agree to do very simple things, lots of them, that all add up to a big difference in terms of actual physical savings in carbon reduction, reduction in global warming, as well as having a tremendous effect and stimulus, motivating and inspiring executives further up the food chain. Ultimately it's all about sharing information, education, spreading the word and building a critical mass of people who are doing the same thing. Sustainability is a problem so large and complex it demands that it be attacked from the bottom up (that's you and me, folks!), as well as top down.

What can we do? Print on both sides of paper, switch computers off, not print emails, buy eBooks and music online, post statements and pay bills online, walk or cycle to work, install LED lighting, use LCD monitors for TV screens, recycle garbage, get a home energy audit, install double glazing, buy organic foods and eat less meat, cover pots while cooking, take a shower instead of a bath, use car sharing, use bottle banks, plant a tree, recycle at home, turn off your car engine when in traffic, fly less, insulate and weatherise your home, buy products that have less packaging, fit energy saving light bulbs, buy a fuel efficient or electric car, drive less - cycle more, fill kettles with the exact amount of water needed, hang out clothes to dry instead of using the tumble dryer, turn down heating by two degrees, turn off TVs and DVD players when not in use, not leave appliances on standby, do weekly shopping in one trip, properly inflate your tyres, insulate lofts and hot water tanks and encourage at least two others to read this book and conserve ....

When more individuals take the initiative and do any of the foregoing (and ideally much more than just one of them) - then the programme for sustainability will be well and truly under way!

There are some very brave far forward-thinking initiatives around the world; for example, a complete futuristic vision put forward by the Zeitgeist movement, based on a resource-based economy:

www.thezeitgeistmovement.com/mission-statement

Mobile phones, the ultimate 'business in a box' and information tool

The mobile phone is truly the ultimate 'business in a box', that can be used on any street corner. It is still the most preferred way for many to share news and information. Mobile phones are also cheaper than a computer to produce and much more easily disposed of or recycled. Lots of innovation, thought and energy is going into making mobile devices greener, more recyclable, longer-lasting and more energy efficient.

Already, in places like Africa, mobile phones outnumber landlines two to one and have become the cornerstone of global economic growth. Often, where there are no shopping malls, paved roads or other amenities, the locals rely on informal roadside convenience stores for all their shopping and supplies. Sometimes the owners run these small businesses from their homes or even mud huts. In days gone by, the shop owner would have to shut up shop for the day and go to the nearest local village to gather supplies. Now, a quick call from the mobile phone ensures they are always fully stocked; soon they will be able to pay for that stock using mobile payment applications, if they don't have a bank account. Studies have already proved that introducing 10 mobile phones per 100 people in a developing country can add as much as one per cent to the GDP growth rate.

The next generation of smartphones are already giving the office computer a run for its money and the war hasn't even started. Many mobile phones these days have superb 8-megapixel or greater cameras, video recording and the ability to play high-quality music (which consumers are already spending £32 billion a year downloading) and the bar is constantly being raised even further. Global positioning satellite tracking (GPS) allows phones to be triangulated from receiving antennae to determine where the caller is.

There are devices available that can charge your phone battery in an emergency, by inserting it into a small mechanical charging device that fits over your index finger. You then twirl the device around for a few minutes, which will give you enough power to enable you to make an emergency phone call. Sagem already has a phone that is solar powered and, looking into the future, it is highly likely that mobile devices may be able to be charged wirelessly via the same networks that carry our mobile signal. Advances in kinetic energy will also give us self-charging phones, in a similar fashion to our self-winding watches. Solar powered cell phone towers are already being installed across India.

You can easily scan two-dimensional quick response codes (QR) and these are beginning to appear on business cards, simplifying the task of entering contact information into address books. This enables sure-fire networking; one good business contact can frequently pay for an entire trip.

Japan leads the world in mobile banking, the use of touch-sensitive technology for credit or debit cards and eTicketing; locals regularly use their phones to pay for soft drinks from vending machines, for subway tokens and miscellaneous other low-cost everyday purchases.

Business applications will abound and often surprise as software improves and arrives: full Internet browsing, video calling, advanced audience polling, surveys, mobile maps, real-time traffic, text broadcasting, satellite imagery, high-quality network conferencing, social networking and more-private social networks, mobile TV and every single application will be so much easier to navigate. Each year brings ever-more powerful information processing packages in smaller, more convenient devices.

Having spent an eventful and expensive five years in the hologram industry, I can confidently predict that, eventually, there will be mobile devices with holographic projection and full three-dimensional rendering that will be invaluable for architects, product designers and salesman; in the fullness of time, the medical profession will be able access full-body holographic images.

Although there are nearly five billion mobile phones on the planet, we haven't really started to leverage and harness the 'awesome mobile devices of the future' for business processes and real-time information; when we do, they will become the driver of economic opportunity and we will begin to change the world. Don't forget, 2015 and 2020 are just around the corner. As I have mentioned on numerous occasions, it's not just the next generation of *devices* that will make a difference, but also the next generation of *users*.

Water, water, everywhere, but...

You are as probably as surprised as I am to find yourself reading about water in a book about information, but hopefully you'll see where I am going with this.

Industrial water usage accounts for up to 88% of all water consumed worldwide; 50% of that is in the United States where over one billion gallons of water is used *each day* in the oil refinement industry, according to the US Department of the Environment. Water is used for just about everything, and it is only recently that we have come to acknowledge that this commodity is being abused and is not perpetually renewable. We must also take into account the billion-plus people globally who do not have access to running water - imagine!

It takes approximately 10 gallons of water to make a single computer chip, which may not appear too much at first blush - but we make billions of them. A typical semiconductor factory makes two million integrated circuits a month, using 20 million gallons of water, which ultimately gets disposed of as waste. Turning silicon wafers into chips requires many steps, including etching, doping, heating and rinsing with clean water between each stage, to remove impurities.

You can see that we need to breed a new type of engineer who will design in environmental factors from the beginning of every manufacturing process - including the most expedient ways to wash chips, and then recycle the water.

Businesses are already coming up with innovative ways to use water and then reuse it, and now treat it with the respect of a valuable commodity; they are developing a greener corporate image into the bargain.

Electricity

To put it into perspective, the global IT industry consumes over $50 billion worth of power every year and the amount is increasing all the time. That's an inordinate amount of carbon emissions and greenhouse gas. Google's 900,000 servers alone consume over 2.3 megawatts and gets an annual bill of around $300 million plus - imagine the sound that bill would make when it comes through the letterbox and hits the doormat!

On a global level, we generate electricity like this: 68% comes from fossil fuels, coal, gas and oil; 13.4% from nuclear fission; and 19% from hydro and other renewable sources such as solar and wind turbine. Currently, there is no tangible evidence that says we can do without any of these.

We now need to encourage children to become champions of energy conservation, and develop and harness *new* ideas in solar, wind, sun, sea, hydrogen, nuclear and - this is important - things we haven't even thought of yet. We do this by getting them to engage with enthusiasm the things that they will love doing; creating solar-driven go-karts, making experiments with the wind and sun, and constantly pointing out the differences between renewable and non-renewable energy sources - emphasising the growing difficulty of finding energy whose supply is ever-decreasing whilst demand continues to grow.

The fact is, the countries where there is a thirst for information that can be turned into knowledge and are doing something about it, are consuming vast amounts of electricity and other resources to make it all happen, putting a major new twist on 'Knowledge is Power': maybe it should be 'Knowledge costs Power'.

Solar

The main role of the Information Overlord is to have an abundance of information, to know where to find that information and how to transmute it into knowledge that can be acted upon. Above everything, he must *share* that knowledge. At this pivotal point in history, sharing information about solar energy is of extreme importance; one day in the future, it could be the primary source of energy that drives information technology, production and dissemination.

Solar energy was harnessed by the Greeks and Chinese hundreds of years ago, by designing their houses so that major windows pointed toward the south. We have now started to harness the sun in many more sophisticated ways, including solar heating, solar architecture and solar thermal electricity. The solar energy reaching our planet is colossus and is about twice as much as will ever be mined from non-renewable sources, such as coal, natural gas and uranium; all of these started life as sunlight, captured by the process of photosynthesis in green plants and trees.

Major solar sustainability initiatives are happening all over the world and these early adopters and early stage 'experiments' should be considered as learning investments and in the interest of the planet; that information and knowledge must be shared.

China, Israel and Cyprus are leading the way on the deployment of solar hot water heating systems. In the United States, Canada and Australia, many homes have swimming pools heated by solar hot water systems. The Sarnia Photovoltaic Power plant in Canada is the largest in the world. Facebook's Menlo Park, California headquarters is outfitted with a solar power system that supplies its fitness centre with electricity and hot water for post-workout showers. Apple has revealed plans to build America's largest private solar panel farm that will cover 100 acres of North Carolina, and produce enough power to supply thousands of homes. Apple will use the eco-power for a huge data centre where the servers for its iTunes and iCloud services are held.

Aggregating information resources for the common good

The technology to harness the power of idle computers has been around for some time now but has yet to be fully exploited, most likely due to a lack of awareness. It's a great way for anyone who owns or uses a computer to share information-processing power to deliver a common goal.

A good example of where this theory has been put into action is GridRepublic (*http://www.gridrepublic.org*) where members run a screensaver that allows their computers to work on public-interest research projects when their machines are not in use. The screensaver does not affect performance of the host computer any more than an ordinary screensaver does.

By aggregating idle resources from PC users around the world, GridRepublic has created, in effect, a massive supercomputer. Computations that would take tens of thousands of years to compute on an ordinary computer can be processed in just a few months. New medicines can be developed, the human genome can be explored, the physical origins of the universe can be modelled and probed, the search for signs of life on other planets can be extended. All these and other questions can be examined in ways never before possible.

If you are unable to turn your computer off at night, this has to be a good way of, at least, utilising the energy you are using, to benefit mankind.

Cloud computing and sustainability

Putting more and more servers out there to cope with the burgeoning amounts of information we are producing - how can this possibly be an environmental benefit, I hear you ask? Accenture carried out a study that suggests there will be a net sustainability benefit, as organisations and businesses embrace 'the Cloud' - large-scale, shared IT infrastructure available over the Internet.

The Cloud's unprecedented economies can reduce overall cost and increase efficiencies, especially when replacing an organisation's locally operated onsite servers. But what of the environmental benefit?

Taking Microsoft as an example, the study found that, for large deployments, Cloud solutions can reduce energy use and carbon emissions by more than 30% when compared to equivalent business applications that were installed onsite.

The benefits were even more impressive for smaller deployments, where energy use and emissions could be reduced by more than 90% when using a shared Cloud service.

How is that possible? Cloud services are hosted in dedicated data centres, which are optimised to save energy by implementing hardware and software solutions that keep its use close to maximum capacity; new resources are added only at the last moment; on the other hand, your normal home and office computers run and consume energy, but are idle quite a lot of the time. Also, Cloud technologies use virtualisation that allows dynamic resource management, so resources can be switched on and off in seconds or even milliseconds when needed, therefore saving a lot of energy during low-demand periods.

The big thing here for me is that to deliver a net environmental benefit from the Cloud, we all have to think hard about how we use our local pieces of IT kit to produce, store and disseminate information. As the Information Overlord, this will require some tough decisions to be made - such as entrusting all of your valuable information and knowledge to a server somewhere in the USA or another far-flung country. Merely keeping copies of everything stored on a local hard drive is only going to exacerbate the situation. Ultimately, the desktop computer as we know it will have to radically change to fully exploit both the economies and efficiencies which Cloud computing has to offer.

Google has already produced a Chrome netbook that, basically, has only their Chrome browser built in, with a very simple OS. You store all your resources in the Cloud, so the netbook can be very cheap. It consumes very little power, and there is not much that can crash or break as the browser itself is the operating system.

Our desktop computers and laptops frequently crash, usually due to bugs resulting from complexity of the various operating systems (such as Windows, or Apple OS), which consist of millions of lines of code. Nobody can test all possible combinations and, if you factor in the installation of other software and hardware drivers, which can add hundreds of thousands *more* lines of code, you can imagine the magnitude of the problem. It's a miracle that those operating systems function at all!

eBooks and eBook readers

eBooks have taken off with remarkable rapidity and the Amazon Kindle, despite stiff competition from all sorts of other mobile devices including Apple iPhone and various tablet devices, still leads the field. In 10 or so years' time, maybe sooner, it will be deemed anti-social to read a newly printed book when you should be in conservation mode, and reading a digital version that doesn't consume carbon-gobbling trees. Kids, nowadays, automatically expect to read information on the screen; just wait until the next few generations come along and everyone will do this as second nature. No one will want to read a printed book, any more than you or I would want to watch a black and white television or watch a silent movie.

Audible

Audible Audiobooks is owned by Amazon and is rapidly changing the way people acquire books and assimilate information in a more environmentally friendly way. Many people prefer to listen to a book passively, whilst on the move, on the subway or driving or walking to work; an audio book is the way to do that. They are also a great way for people with blindness or impaired sight to keep up to date with the latest bestseller or business information publication.

Sustainability has introduced hundreds of commercial opportunities to businesses and entrepreneurs; many of the sectors we have discussed I am, or have been, already involved with, directly or indirectly. Some of these topics have just 'arrived upon us' without us being fully conscious as to why but, in the broader scheme of things, they are all part of the 'sustainability package' and overall opportunity.

The biggest legacy of all

We will leave as our legacy, information and information technology that will ultimately, if in the hands of the Information Overlord, create knowledge. That knowledge will lead to the creation of new ways of producing sustainable energy and more environmentally friendly methods of dealing with information and information overload.

ZOOM SECRETS

Your Personal Action Plan (12)

In a world of information overload, creating sustainability is a massive challenge; however, it is one that we are well-suited to embrace

Knowledge sharing and training is the one area in which the Information Overlord can make an immediate, positive difference to the effect that information overload has on our environment.

The solution is quite simple and commercially beneficial as well as environmentally friendly. People simply need to be trained in, fully understand and have a list of practical things to action every day that will lessen the negative effect that information production, dissemination and storage can have on the world's resources.

Consider putting in place some or all of the following practical ideas in your business or organisation to move forward your sustainability agenda:

1. *Create a long-term sustainability strategy that will integrate with your IT and marketing strategies - consider appointing a Chief Sustainability Officer to drive that strategy forward.*

2. *Educate yourself and your colleagues/employees about the impact information, technology and the Internet has on our environment.*

3. Implement basic green rules in the company such as recycling, double-side and low-quality printing by default, turning down the heating etc.

4. Analyse potential savings from optimising your server rooms and data centres, or by migrating to the Cloud.

5. Replace paper document creation and storing with digital documents.

6. Shout about your green successes and share with others to help them learn from you.

7. Become a sustainability champion in your function or industry.

8. Above all, monitor your sustainability performance and constantly update your strategy as new environmentally friendly solutions become available.

CHAPTER 13

FACETS OF INFORMATION

"Like a Diamond, Information has many Facets"

Ron G Holland

Information about Information

This book has been all about information and this final chapter aims to close a few loops and stimulate your mind into moving in a few more directions that you may not have previously considered. The masses are creating vast piles of information, but there are very few people collating, adding value and presenting it in an understandable format - a format that can actually be assimilated and ultimately, enable decisions to be made from the insights it uncovers.

This can be hugely valuable because a tiny piece of information can often prove to be the missing link or final piece in a puzzle that may give you competitive advantage, solve a problem or assist in your fundraising or marketing programme. Knowing where something was, or how it performed, or how it interacted with you, can often be worth more than the item itself.

The Information Overlord knows that frequently, little pieces of seemingly insignificant information, can come from obscure sources; it frequently takes a number of these pieces to click into place before you receive your fully blown Eureka! This final chapter is designed to help you find any missing pieces, in order to help you become a fully qualified Information Overlord. Enjoy this part of the journey. As Churchill said, "It is not the end of the beginning, but it is the beginning of the end."

Information warfare

I can imagine quite a few people getting to this chapter and immediately jumping to the conclusion, "None of this pertains to me..." - and how wrong they would be. The only time they may wake up to what is happening is when someone steals their identity, hacks into their bank account or when they try to access some information on their computer and some bug, Trojan or virus has corrupted it or made it disappear altogether. Occasionally things will happen and you may well be totally oblivious; most cybercrime is undetectable, and that is part and parcel of information warfare.

On a national and international level, all modern societies are at risk; none more so than in the areas of information, electricity distribution, finance, water, communication and transportation infrastructures. The whole kit and caboodle is backed up by power, predominantly electricity. Take out the electricity and you quickly plummet nations back into the dark ages - quite literally.

Information infrastructures are so important these days and become more so as each moment passes. In recent years, we saw US and British forces take out the entire network of communications on the first night of the Gulf War, in a mission aptly christened, 'Shock and Awe'. The US Air Force has had Information Warfare Squadrons since the 1980s and its mission is to fly, fight and win - in air, space and cyberspace.

Already highly sophisticated direct energy weapons exist, such as High Energy Radio Frequency guns and Electromagnetic Pulse bombs that can disable and destroy electricity systems very effectively.

On a commercial level the Information Overlord may want to drill down into a niche area and become an expert in that area alone. The areas of banking, finance, transportation, computer security, communication and military already employ armies of people who keep the bad guys out - but there is always room for one more specialist who can provide a quantum leap and an added layer of protection.

On a personal level, the Information Overlord has to be on high alert and protect him or herself at all times, by all means: guard pin numbers when using ATMs; don't leave pin numbers in your wallet; don't trash any papers (no matter how seemingly unimportant) without shredding them first; use powerful anti-virus software - much of which you can download for free; ensure your firewall is activated; check online bank accounts regularly and report even tiny anomalies immediately; have really strong passwords on *all* your computers; consider encrypting all your data (a password alone will not protect your data well - only encryption gives a high level of protection against a theft of your computer); ensure your children are well-protected on the computers and sites they use; never put your real date of birth and address details on social media sites. If you sell or give your computer away to a friend or charity, make sure you get the hard drive professionally 'cleaned' beforehand - or preferably removed and destroyed, if you are at all unsure as to how accessible your personal information might be to a potential criminal.

The most frightening thing about Information Warfare is that you don't see it until it hits you and sometimes you don't see it all, ever.

Intellectual Property Office, formerly The Patent Office

Throughout this book, you have hopefully become increasingly aware that information can have massive value; in many cases it needs to be formally protected from the competition. When you come up with your own Eureka! or a corporation comes up with an idea, it sometimes pays to get that information protected. However, Intellectual Property law is notoriously confusing and is surrounded by myths.

In the UK, the place to go is the Intellectual Property Office if you want to patent specific information about products, inventions and ideas; in the U.S. it is the United States Patent and Trademark Office.

Big corporations register thousands of patents in order to protect what they have invented; in 2010 the United States filed 44,855 applications, Japan 32,156 and the UK 15,490.

The origins of patents in the UK stretch back well over 400 years but the Patent Office was formally established in 1852 as the sole office for protecting information about products and inventions. It is interesting to note that, when you lodge a patent, it has to be information that is new, not obvious and capable of being made or used in some kind of industry. You can't lodge patents that are mathematical discovery, literary or musical or arts, ways of doing business or presenting information and many other things.

Over the years, I have had some involvement with patents; my own hologram book, car anti-theft devices, smart cards and floating doorsteps are the ones that spring to mind. It costs time and money to patent a product or technology and of course you must bear in mind that only a miniscule percentage of patents lodged ever see the light of day in the commercial world and make money for their owners.

You really do need to evaluate whether you need a patent or not, and conduct some diligent research as to what patents already exist around your own particular idea, information and technology. Sometimes the best advice would be: get on with it and try to turn your idea into commercial reality and make some money. I say this because I have seen so many projects get bogged down with the process, succeeded in getting the application and then spent years paying the fees to keep the patent alive and the entrepreneurs themselves never made a penny because they were just focused on the patent process and not on the business of making money.

Only recently we have seen Facebook battle with rival Yahoo over technology patents. It is highly likely that if Facebook doesn't start paying licensing fees soon, they will be sued. No one is exempt: Apple had big problems with Nokia, Microsoft had problems with Uniloc and eBay with MercExchange.

Each year companies pay out millions of pounds to inventors who have great products, ideas and inventions; but my best advice is to talk to a number of people who have been through the patent minefield - as well as a few good patent lawyers and a number of 'patent gurus' who can handhold you through the whole patent process. By talking to lots of people you will then be able to make an informed decision, with your eyes wide open, as to how you want to proceed in the protection of your information. As they recommend in the military, if you have to go through a minefield, make sure you follow someone.

Freedom of Information Act

Freedom of Information is not a new concept and dates back to Sweden's Freedom of Press Act of 1766, which is the oldest in the world.

The current Freedom of Information legislation in the UK comprises laws that guarantee the general public have access to data held by the state and usually excludes data held by private individuals.

Data

You may want to consider that data is at the lowest, most granular level from whence information is derived. Computers and people gather data; once you have that information you can then transmute it into usable knowledge. Data, on its own, carries no meaning; it must be interpreted and then take on a meaning. For example, let's consider data about the deepest part of the ocean. That data may include the depth of the ocean in metres. Now consider a book containing all the characteristics of the ocean including currents, rip tides, water pressure and darkness. This would be considered information. Then consider the best approach to safely reach the ocean floor - that may be considered knowledge.

Data Protection Act

This is a UK act that is long and complex and is primarily aimed at companies, rather than individuals, who hold and store data on other people. Over the years it has been honed and refined; because of EC directives it now means, for example, that Internet marketers capturing anything more than a name and an email address from customers (such as address, telephone number and credit card details) have to fully abide by the Data Protection Act. For the end consumer, this is great news because the Act is there as an additional safety net, helping to protect us when we give our credit card details to a business over the telephone or Internet, safeguarding against potential card detail abuse by the retailer.

The data protection act consists of eight basic principles and here they are, broken down into very simplistic terms:

1. You may only use the data for the purpose it was collated

2. You must not disclose the data to third parties

3. Individuals have the right to view data you have acquired

4. You may not keep the data longer than necessary

5. You may not send the data outside the European Economic Area

6. All companies that use data and process personal information, must register with the Information Commissioner's Office

7. You must have safety measures in place which include staff training and keeping the information safe. On the technical side, you must have sufficient firewalls in place to protect data from unwanted external intrusions.

8. Individuals have the right to have factually *incorrect* information corrected

Information Commissioner's Office

The Information Commissioner's Office (ICO) is an independent public body set up to promote access to official information and to protect personal information. It deals with the Data Protection Act, the Private and Electronic Communications Regulations, the Freedom of Information Act and the Environmental Information Regulations and its mission is to: 'uphold information rights in the public interest, promoting openness by public bodies and data privacy for individuals.'

Classified Information

Most governments have a way of classifying information that needs different levels of clearance before an individual can access it. At the top of the list would be 'Top Secret', which is material that could possibly cause 'exceptionally grave damage' to national security were it to be made public. Further down the list come 'Secret', 'Confidential', 'Restricted' and, last but not least, 'Unrestricted'. Government information about nuclear weapons, for example, frequently carries further marking to show the material contains such information.

Corporations also engage in protecting sensitive information; although, in the US, the Employees' Polygraph Protection Act prevents corporations requesting employees (or even potential employees) to take polygraph tests, background checks are frequently carried out on individuals with whom it will be associating. Corporations use many levels of classifying information so that only cleared and qualified individuals can access it; 'For your eyes only', 'In professional confidence' and 'Confidential' are just a few of the labels used.

Information with value can sometimes be world changing. I remember reading a story way back, when Steve Jobs was developing the Apple Macintosh, of how he went to extraordinary lengths to keep all his employees separate from each other, and for them to only be working on applications they were briefed on - and to keep that information strictly under wraps. Only when the Mac was finished were the mouse, 'drag and drop', and a host of other revolutionary mind-blowing technologies revealed to the waiting press and public. At around the same time, I read another story of how Sabeer Bhatia and Jack Smith kept their information secret about their free email offering, right up until the day of launch; and how they put the name HoTMaiL on the office door on that day. Their secrecy obviously paid off, as it was bought by Microsoft about a year later for an estimated $400 million and then rebranded MSN Hotmail (now part of Live.com).

This is something you may want to take on board when you tell your employees everything about your business - because they are just as likely to go off and try to do it for themselves. It may pay dividends to keep things on a 'need to know' basis only and to keep projects separate. Good practice would also suggest having in place a robust signed non-disclosure contract, to help secure your company's valuable intellectual property.

Copyright

Plagiarism is often claimed to be the highest form of flattery - however I am sure that many authors who have suffered as a result of outright copying of their works, would clearly challenge this. By all means, don't let other's work evade your eyes - learn from it and then develop your own unique offering and make sure you adhere to copyright law.

Copyright is an automatic right and comes into play whenever an individual or business creates a piece of work. That work however, must be regarded as being original as well as clearly showing elements of labour, skill or judgement.

Copyright interpretation is specific to the individual creation, rather than the *idea* behind the creation. For example, an idea for a book would not in itself be protected, but the content of the book would be. What that actually means is that someone else is entitled to write their own book around the same idea, on the proviso that they do not directly copy or adapt the book to do so.

Names, titles, short phrases and colours are not normally included within the interpretation - but a logo design that combines all of these elements almost certainly would be.

If you or your business needs to share information that is bound by copyright, a copyright licence can be easily obtained, but check out any limitations first. If your organisation holds a licence, as the Information Overlord will know, communicating how that licence works with all employees within the business is essential, otherwise holding one becomes a pointless exercise! The best everyday example is that of copying newspaper articles or pages from journals, within your office. You need a formal licence to do this.

Information Visualisation

Having been an author of right and left-brain thinking books for over 30 years, and encouraging my readers to think in pictures as much as they do in words, this topic is not only right up my street but deserves some serious delving into and discussion.

If you've seen websites such as, 'Digg Big Spy' (which now seems to be deceased but still worth viewing) 'We Feel Fine', 'GapMinder', or 'InformationIsBeautiful' and you're a Web surfer, you are probably amazed at what you have been viewing.

Information Visualisation has been born out of computer graphics and their use in their early stages of development to solve and study scientific problems. It has the advantage of being able to engage the human eye's broad bandwidth pathway into the mind and allow you to see the big picture of even the most complex subject in the most simplistic way - concurrently.

I must confess that I have never really had the slightest interest in politics until I stumbled on the Information is Beautiful visualisation of 'How politics works'; within three seconds I understood the subject from top to bottom. The cork nearly popped out the top of my head. I printed it off and rushed around the office showing it to various colleagues. They were also stunned and grasped the concept of politics within seconds.

Information Visualisation is now being used extensively in many areas including scientific research, crime mapping, data mining, digital libraries, market studies and financial data analysis.

ZOOM SECRETS

Your Personal Action Plan (13)

Little pieces of seemingly insignificant information can come from obscure sources; it frequently takes a number of these pieces to click into place before you receive your fully blown Eureka!

Time invested to focus on the validation, quality, security and use of small pieces of important information will pay dividends in the long-term

Take action to:

1. *Protect your IP from the very beginning - work with IP lawyers from a reputable company.*

2. *Comply with the Data Protection Act and register with the appropriate body if you handle customers' sensitive data.*

3. *Identify areas which should be kept secret from employees who don't need to know about them and put confidentiality agreements in place.*

4. *Treat copyrights seriously - don't use content to which you don't have rights and consult lawyers before publishing anything that has someone else's material.*

5. *Hire an ethical hacker to test your organisation's defences.*

CONCLUSION

I am reminded of a series of tests done on some poor frogs. The first frog was dropped into a bowl of very hot water and he immediately hopped out as fast as he could. The second frog was slowly lowered into a bowl of lukewarm water and the heat gradually increased until he boiled to death.

I fear that the machines have already taken over and like the frog that slowly got boiled to death, information overload has crept up on us in stealth mode...and most of us never saw it coming.

I know of only one antidote and that is a very powerful one. Take back the reins of your life and business and attain total peace of mind by *becoming an Information Overlord*. To enable this transition to take place, you will need to first master the art of Mind Power.

To do that is simple – but not easy. You need to take time out in Silence, Stillness and Solitude ($$$) and indulge in both no-mind and also the visualisation of the goals you are trying to attain.

Become more inaccessible and don't let other people's emails (i.e. other people's agendas) overwhelm you. If you follow these simple instructions, you will begin to increase your personal power, reduce stress in your life and increase your happiness - and after all, that's what it should be all about, yes? Take these simple steps and you will master the information age and in doing so, you WILL become an Information Overlord!

THE INFORMATION OVERLORD'S TOOLKIT

I have carefully selected a number of really useful information management tools that I hope you will be able to put to good use every day, both at home and in the office. Visit my website www.RonGHolland.com for regular updates. In the meantime, here are a few of the ones I love, which were all available at the time of going to press, to get you started:

File Sharing:

- **Dropbox** – Perfect for sharing files and collaborating. **www.dropbox.com**

- **WeTransfer** – Online service for sending large files via email. **www.wetransfer.com**

- **Google Docs (also named Google Drive)** – Create or upload documents and files and share them privately or publicly. **www.docs.google.com**

- **YouTube (Video Sharing)** – Online service for sharing and playing videos privately or publicly. **www.youtube.com**

- **Attachments.me** – Facilitates file sharing straight from your online email account (selected providers only). **www.attachments.me**

- **Amazon S3 – Simple Storage Service** – File storage for advanced users, mainly businesses. **www.aws.amazon.com/s3/**

Collaboration and Blogging:

- **Google Docs (Google Drive)** – Create documents and work on them with other people at the same time. **www.docs.google.com**

- **WordPress** – Blogging and website platform with easy to use back office. **www.wordpress.com**

- **Zimbra** – Email and Collaboration – An enterprise-class email, calendar and collaboration solution, built for the cloud, both public and private. **www.zimbra.com**

Online Calendars:

- **Google Calendar** – Online calendar, can be synced with smartphone and various other applications. **www.google.com/calendar/**

Task Management:

- **Remember The Milk** – Simple and very clever online task management tool. **www.rememberthemilk.com**

- **Simpleology** – Well-structured online task management system with efficiency courses and other tools based on science of performance. **www.simpleology.com**

Event Management and Marketing:

- **Eventbrite** – Create and manage events online. **www.eventbrite.com**

- **Facebook** – Create and promote events online. **www.facebook.com**

- **Google Plus** – Create and promote events online. **www.plus.google.com**

Mass Mailing:

- **MailChimp** – Professional email lists and campaign management tools. **www.mailchimp.com**

- **GetResponse** – As above. **www.getresponse.co.uk**

- **phpList (for technically advanced users)** – A simple, effective tool, it's free if you install it on your own server/hosting account. **www.phplist.com**

CRM - Customer Relationship Marketing

- **Infusionsoft (CRM)** – All in one automated marketing system. (Contact us to see how we can help you with this.) **www.infusionsoft.com**

- **1ShoppingCart** – All in one shopping cart. **www.1shoppingcart.com**

Merchant/Ecommerce Services

- **Sage Pay** – Merchant services for business. **www.sagepay.com**

- **Zettle** – Taking card payments. **www.izettle.com**

- **GoCardless** – Simple direct debit. **www.gocardless.com**

Accounting System

- **Xero** – Accounting software for Businesses. **www.xero.com/uk**

Productivity

- **Evernote** – Ultimate tool for note keeping across all devices. **www.evernote.com**

Payroll

- **Sage** – Cloud Payroll: **www.uk.sageone.com/payroll/**

Get free downloads and find out more about Ron G Holland's latest publications, mentoring and business ventures at:
www.RonGHolland.com

www.ingramcontent.com/pod-product-compliance
Lightning Source LLC
Chambersburg PA
CBHW050129170426
43197CB00011B/1763